Trade, Investment and Competition in International Banking

Trade, Investment and Competition in International Banking

Aidan O'Connor

palgrave
macmillan

First published 2005 by
PALGRAVE MACMILLAN
Houndmills, Basingstoke, Hampshire RG21 6XS and
175 Fifth Avenue, New York, N. Y. 10010
Companies and representatives throughout the world

PALGRAVE MACMILLAN is the global academic imprint of the Palgrave Macmillan division of St. Martin's Press, LLC and of Palgrave Macmillan Ltd.
Macmillan® is a registered trademark in the United States, United Kingdom and other countries. Palgrave is a registered trademark in the European Union and other countries.

ISBN-13: 978–1–4039–4132–9 hardback
ISBN-10: 1–4039–4132–7 hardback

This book is printed on paper suitable for recycling and made from fully managed and sustained forest sources.

A catalogue record for this book is available from the British Library.

Library of Congress Cataloging-in-Publication Data
O'Connor, Aidan, 1955–
Trade, investment, and competition in international banking / by Aidan O'Connor.
p. cm.
Includes bibliographical references and index.
ISBN 1–4039–4132–7
1. Banks and banking, International. 2. International finance. I. Title.

HG3881.O268 2005
332.1′5–dc22 2005047293

10 9 8 7 6 5 4 3 2 1
14 13 12 11 10 09 08 07 06 05

Printed and bound in Great Britain by
Antony Rowe Ltd, Chippenham and Eastbourne

To the memory of my father
and
For my mother

Contents

List of Tables

List of Figures

Acknowledgements

Writing a book depends on many people and organisations for its completion. While those who assisted me are too numerous to mention I must acknowledge the support of the many scholars and organisations that supplied books, journals, articles or research papers.

In particular, I must acknowledge the support of the various academic libraries, and the many helpful librarians, who allowed me access to their resources. The generosity of all astounded me.

I am most grateful to several people at Palgrave, to Rebecca Pash, Assistant Editor for her efficiency during the administration of the project, to Stephen Rutt, Publishing Director, for his prompt response to my proposal which encouraged me enormously, and finally to Jacky Kippenberger, Commissioning Editor, for her patience and advice in managing the process.

Aidan O'Connor
France
July 2005

Introduction

There are three distinct eras in the development of financial systems. These are the pre-modern era up to the early 18th century, the modern era from the early 18th century to the mid 20th century and thereafter the contemporary era, an extension of modern banking and which may be subdivided into the Bretton Woods era 1945–1973 and the post-Bretton Woods or floating exchange rates era.

The beginning of modern financial systems is considered as the early 18th century in western Europe, the late 18th century in the rest of Europe and the Americas, the 19th century in south and east Asia, Australia and Oceania and the early 20th century in sub-Saharan Africa. A reason for such a lag in the development of systems between regions is due to the criteria used in defining a modern financial system. The features of a modern financial system are considered as a monetised sector, fiduciary money issued either by a central bank or by banks acting in such a capacity, and limited liability private firms.[1]

The international financial system comprises private banks, public monetary authorities and international financial institutions. The focus is on private international banks, that is, commercial, investment and universal banks.

The development and evolution of international banking includes structural developments, in terms of size, scope, products and processes, in terms of the legal and regulatory systems and also in terms of the business activities of banks.

The central theme is trade and investment in the international banking industry, the main aspects of which are cross-border trade in banking services, foreign direct investment by banks, international financial centres, capital movements and competition between banks. This theme is treated from evolutionary and theoretical aspects, as well as, from the competitive aspects of the leading international banks. The international banking industry is treated from the perspective of regulations, markets and banks and their inter-relations and the increased competition and internationalisation of the industry.

The first part traces the evolution and development of international banking through the development of national banking industries, international financial centres and international banks in the pre-modern banking era and in the modern era up to the 1950s. This historical overview is primarily country based to reflect the nature of the development of banking in different countries and the evolution and development of international financial centres in specific locations. While of necessity selective it is a representative overview of the evolution of banking.

The second part focuses on the characteristics and influences on international banking in the contemporary banking era. There is an emphasis on innovations in markets, products and processes and their rapid and widespread diffusion, thereby accelerating the integration of international banking. Due to the pivotal role of banking in an economy, banks have been highly regulated, thus shaping national banking and the ability of banks to operate internationally. There is also a focus on de-regulation and liberalisation of banking markets, mergers and acquisitions and capital movements. The influence of international trade agreements and international bank regulation is also outlined.

The third part outlines the main theories of international trade and foreign direct investment and their application to cross-border trade in banking services and to foreign direct investment by banks. There is also an analysis of international financial centres and the business activities of banks in these centres. This part also classifies contemporary international banking by type of bank, service, and customer.

Competitive advantage by international banks is the theme of the fourth part and outlines the organisation and activities of selected international banks and analyses the competitive aspects of international banks to ascertain the leading banks based on the quality of their services and international orientation.

Part five reviews the evolution, the current state of international banking and the strategies of international banks.

Part I

The Evolution and Development of International Banking

Part I

1

International Banking in the Pre-Modern and Modern Banking Eras

Trade was centred in fairs in medieval times and it was there that money-changing type banking services commenced. Fairs were held at regular intervals and developed as meeting places for merchants from many regions. They differed from markets as they were held less frequently, although regularly, and continued for a few weeks. These fairs were often centred on wholesale trade between merchants and developed into financial centres where bankers established branches.

This is the earliest form of international banking and the trade fair the earliest form of financial centre. These centres emerged in places that were strategically situated on the main trade routes and flourished due to their local patronage and to the protection provided for foreigners. Their emergence was associated with trade, their development associated with innovation and advances in financial systems and their decline with politics, especially in the pre-modern and the early modern banking eras.

Developments in northern Italy

North Italian bankers were the earliest bankers in the modern sense, the term 'bank' deriving from *banca,* the Italian for bench. North Italian cities such as Florence, Lucca, Siena, Genoa and Venice flourished in oriental trade between the 12th and 15th centuries. Money-changing type of banking existed because of the many different denominations of coins that circulated freely. As these coins contained a specific amount of precious metal they were easily convertible.

Banking also developed from merchants who financed foreign trade. The emergence of merchant bankers occurred in the 13th century when the bill of exchange was developed. This was one of the most influential innovations in banking and allowed merchants, instead of accompanying goods to fairs and markets themselves, to send representatives or use local correspondents. The merchant banks of Florence and Lucca were to the forefront in its application.[1] With its widespread use in Europe, the bill of exchange became the main form of trade finance.

Representative offices soon emerged in the leading trade centres and these later developed into branches. It was the banking dynasties of northern Italy which were influential up until the 16th century that were to the forefront in transforming banks from trade fair representative offices to those with permanent branches. These banks had branches throughout Europe and were also sources of information on trade conditions for the bankers. By 1335, the Pedruzzi bankers, had branches throughout Italy and Europe, with five agents in England, four in France, four in Flanders, four at Avignon and 11 in the Kingdom of Naples. Outside shareholders of the Pedruzzi bank were by this time in the majority.[2] Branches were mostly managed by relatives and their capital was composed of the partners' own funds although some were managed by agents. The Florentine, Bardi and Pedruzzi bankers managed their bank as a joint stock company.[3] These bankers began to lend to sovereigns, many of whom were unable or unwilling to repay, and this led to the closure of some of the banks.

The trade fairs were not without political influence. The fair at Geneva emerged when mainly Italian merchants and bankers moved there. Louis XI of France forbade French merchants from attending this fair and an alternative fair was established at Lyon. With the transfer of some of the merchants and bankers from Geneva to Lyon in 1465, it became the leading financial centre in France until Paris assumed that role. The Genoans were prohibited from attending the fair at Lyon and so established a fair at Besançon, a free city, and in the 16th century this was an internationally important financial centre. Fairs declined in importance by the 17th century.[4]

Northern Europe

Bruges was one of the most important money markets in north-western Europe in the 14th and 15th centuries and north Italian bankers established branches there. A *buerse*, or the current term 'bourse', was established there, the term originating from that of the Van der Buerse inn.[5] Between the 14th and 16th centuries other important financial centres developed in Europe, such as Augsburg and Antwerp. Frankfurt was a leading financial centre in central Europe due to its links with the Lyon, Besançon and Piacenza fairs. The decline of northern Italy as the most important centre of banking commenced with the decline of the Florentine bankers in the early 16th century and continued with the decline of Genoa as a trading centre a century later. One of the reasons for this was the opening of new sea routes to the east around the Cape of Good Hope with the sea faring Dutch and Portuguese becoming the leading traders with the orient. The Atlantic economy also increasingly gained importance for these traders, as well as for the English.

South Germany, especially the city of Augsburg, which was easily accessible from northern Italy, became a leading banking centre and the Fuggers, the Welsers and the Hochstetters were the most important bankers in the 16th century. They were involved in international commodity trade, foreign exchange and sovereign lending.[6] The Fuggers financed the House of Hapsburg and helped ensure the election of Charles V as Holy Roman Emperor. They had branches throughout Europe like their northern Italian counterparts before them. Also like some of the north Italian bankers, sovereign lending in the 1550s eventually brought about their closure due to defaults on loans. Augsburg as a centre of banking did not last very long but it had a lasting influence on the banking industry as banks there developed the concept of financial intermediation by accepting deposits for sovereign lending.[7]

Antwerp emerged as an international financial centre in the late 15th and early 16th centuries and was also a leading centre for international trade in the first half of the 16th century. The endorsing of bills of exchange began there on a large scale in 1600, although there had been endorsing on a limited scale in northern Italy since the 14th century. This rendered the instrument negotiable. Another development was the discounting of bills of exchange thereby making it possible to sell a claim.[8] This innovation later led to payments with paper banknotes. A bourse was opened there in 1531. It was in Antwerp that the Spanish raised finance and the Portuguese sold their produce. The English, who always had strong trade links with this area, and all the major Augsburg bankers as well as the Genoan bankers, were represented there. It was the credit surpluses, the volume of international trade and the accessibility to capital through a bourse that led to Antwerp becoming the leading financial centre of the period.[9]

The idea and model for an exchange, based on that in Antwerp, was brought to England by the royal exchanger, Sir Thomas Gresham, who had been based there to arrange loans for the crown. Eventually this led to the founding of the Royal Exchange in London in 1571.[10] Banking in the United Kingdom does not have its origins in money-changing type services, as in continental Europe, as this service was managed by the state. Antwerp's decline commenced when it was blockaded, first by the Dutch in 1572 and later by the Spanish in 1585. This and other political events motivated merchants to move to Amsterdam during the 80 years war 1568–1648, although it continued to be an important centre until the late 17th century. Some of these Antwerp merchants also moved to London.

Location, innovation, politics, wars and financial crises were factors in the emergence, development, decline and transition of financial centres from one location to another in the pre-modern era, and these factors would continue to affect financial centres in the modern banking era.

Amsterdam and the onset of modern banking

Amsterdam was the leading financial centre in Europe by the early 17th century. This was due to the availability of capital, a convertible currency, and also its financial system included a commodity exchange and insurance services. The Amsterdam Wisselbank was founded in 1609, styled on the Venetian Banco della Piazza di Rialto which had been founded in 1587. It matched its liabilities with specie, settled bills of exchange and provided highly developed trade finance services. It also developed futures and options business, this business activity being termed *windhandel,* trade in air. Interest rates in the United Provinces were the lowest in the world from the mid 17th to the mid 18th centuries principally due to a high savings rate and the repatriation of profits of the Dutch East India Company.[11] Amsterdam was the base of origin of this company, the largest in the world at that time. One of the most important innovations in finance was that of the shifting to a permanent share capital base by this company, rather than raising temporary share capital for each expedition.

As Amsterdam was at the centre of the main trading routes it dominated international trade and was an entrepôt for capital and information on trade with the East, the Atlantic and the Baltic. It was the leading financial centre in the 17th and 18th centuries despite financial crises in the mid 18th century and four wars with the United Kingdom. One of the reasons for the longevity of Amsterdam as an international financial centre was agglomeration as those related types of financial institutions usually associated with contemporary international financial centres were established there. Although trade was an important factor in the development of Amsterdam as an international financial center, the link between trade and finance began to separate by the late 17th century.[12] The Wisselbank went bankrupt largely due to lending to the Dutch East India Company in the late 18th century when it was in direct competition with the British East India Company although it continued until 1819 when it was liquidated following the founding of the Nederlandsche Bank in 1814 as an issuing bank.[13]

Amsterdam peaked as the leading international financial centre in 1730, but continued to be important until the fourth Anglo-Dutch War in 1780. In the 1780s Dutch investors shifted from the United Kingdom, on the verge of industrial revolution, to France, soon to experience political revolution. Following the revolution of 1789 in France, Dutch investments there were withheld and in 1795 French troops occupied the United Provinces and continued to do so during the Napoleonic Wars. During this period Amsterdam was unable to maintain its position as the centre of international trade routes. The post-Napoleonic political landscape also meant that London was in a prime position to become the leading centre for international trade and finance.

The United Kingdom emerges as the leading creditor country

London bankers had adopted many of the innovations of Antwerp as some of the bankers had migrated from there in the late 16th century. In addition, there were strong links between London and Antwerp in trade and in finance. While Amsterdam had also imported these financial innovations and had enhanced them, it was in London that the basis for the modern banking system of deposit, issuing and discount was developed.[14] At the turn of the 17th century bankers mainly discounted bills of exchange and most of their business was domestic. Foreign business was the domain of the foreign bankers, mostly Italian and Dutch. These bankers were the original merchant bankers. Goldsmiths only became bankers in the 17th century by issuing receipts for gold and these receipts later circulating, led to discounting and endorsing. Private bankers used to be termed merchant or goldsmith bankers depending on their business origins.

When the English crown was in financial difficulty many of the goldsmith bankers were unwilling to lend to it on an individual basis. Instead they formed a consortium, which was initially only a temporary device, but which was the stimulus for an Act of Parliament creating the Bank of England in 1694. It was founded as a joint-stock bank and business people and the nobility purchased shares in the bank along with many foreign investors such as the city of Utrecht, the city of Geneva, and the city and canton of Bern.[15]

During the 19th century the United Kingdom was the leading country in the industrial revolution. This was not only a period of innovations in technical and mechanical processes. There were also innovations in services, especially in the banking industry. Banking comprised of the Bank of England, private banks and country banks, that is, banks outside London. These country banks linked the provinces with London and were an important source of funds for the London capital market, as well as, satisfying the demand for capital by domestic industry. Cheques and bills of exchange circulated as methods of payment and as substitutes for currency. In 1825 there was a crisis among the country banks and in 1826 the Banking Co-Partnership Act authorised joint-stock banks to issue notes outside a 65-mile radius of London. This led to the expansion of rural banking and further funds for investment. There were approximately 100 joint-stock banks in England and Wales prior to the Bank Charter and the Joint-Stock Bank Acts of 1844. Although these reformed the banking system, there was a restriction on the establishment of additional banks until the law was amended in 1857.

The banking system was very efficient. The joint-stock banks tended to be domestically focused while the merchant banks were more international in their business. The merchant bankers specialised in specific activities, such as accepting bills, while bill brokers discounted bills, and this was closely linked to financing international trade. The bill on London, the most important means of international payment, was transformed from a counterpart financial instrument in international trade to a pure financial instrument transaction.[16]

It was the norm for international trade to be financed in London in sterling even when the trading parties, the trade itself or the transportation did not involve the United Kingdom. In addition, a peculiarly British form of bank developed, termed an overseas bank, where the head office was located in London to access the capital market but the business of the bank was conducted outside the United Kingdom. This type of banking was later also developed by French and German bankers.

The United Kingdom was a borrower up until the early 19th century, but from the end of the Napoleonic Wars it began to lend internationally on a large scale. The end of the wars ushered in a period of world economic development and also free trade agreements that had most-favoured-nation clauses. This free trade policy extended to the British Empire. France, the other main European economy, also had similar trade agreements, although its most-favoured-nation clause was rescinded in the late 19th century.[17]

Innovations in transport and communications were important factors in world economic growth and opportunities for foreign investment. Railway transport had commenced in the United Kingdom in 1826 and spread around the world. Railway construction was an important sector for investment from the 1840s, domestically and in continental Europe, the United States, Latin America and the colonies. In the first half of the 19th century British foreign investment was directed to Latin America and to the *ante-bellum* southern states of the United States. Following revolutions in Europe in the mid 19th century and later the Franco-Prussian War in 1870, investment shifted from continental Europe and was mostly directed towards Canada, Australia and New Zealand as well as a renewed interest in Latin America. The United Kingdom was the leading capital exporter due to its trade in raw materials and in the export of its produce, and also due to shipping, banking and insurance services. Its foreign investments also ensured that the balance of payments was positive. London was the world's capital and information centre and the Empire's trade surpluses were deposited there, thereby providing additional capital for investment.

Between 1870 and 1913 foreign lending was 5.7% of the United Kingdom's gross national product annually while in France it was between 2% and 3% and in Germany less than 2%. The returns abroad were usually higher than available domestically. The earnings from those investments amounted to 5.3% of gross domestic product per annum between 1870 and 1913 and tended to exceed new foreign investments. By 1914, the gross nominal value of its foreign assets amounted to between 40% and 50% of its total foreign assets.[18] Its foreign lending was rarely linked to official trade policies, though there were instances, unlike the more frequent practice of this in France and Germany. Neither did the government interfere in disputes between bondholders and foreign governments as it considered the investors to be acting in a private capacity. Only when bonds were issued under government guarantee or when there was an international incident that affected claims did the government intervene.[19]

London was the leading international financial centre. The United Kingdom was the leading trading nation, an advocate of free trade and the leading creditor country. The only other significant creditor country was France and then only from the mid 19th century.

France as a competitor creditor country

In 1801, France was the wealthiest country in Europe although French per capita income was less than half of that of the United Kingdom's. The larger French population and the exclusion of agricultural produce from the data, especially as the United Kingdom was more industrialised and more urbanised, partly explain this. By 1872 national income rankings were reversed when France's net national income was 83% of that in the United Kingdom, though French per capita income had improved to 75% of that of the United Kingdom.[20] During this period the United Kingdom also had a higher average growth rate of per capita gross domestic product.

The French banking system was very international due to the diaspora of Huguenots to such places as Geneva and Amsterdam from the late 17th century. This network of international bankers was referred to as '*la haute banque*'. During the *Ancien Régime* many foreign bankers were attracted to France because of the demand for capital. These private bankers were also heavily involved in financing foreign trade. Banking was by this time centred in Paris whereas Lyon had previously been the principal centre of finance. When France required capital to finance its political expansion most of the banks were unable to lend such large amounts due to their size. This led to the founding of the Banque de France, in 1800. Part of its capital was obtained by subsuming the Caisse des Comptes Courants and part of it by public subscription. The Caisse d'Escompte, a note issuing bank, became part of the Banque de France in 1802. The French banking system was not very well developed in the first half of the 19th century. The Banque de France and the *hautes banques* resisted attempts to establish note issue banks outside Paris, thereby preventing the development of banking in the provinces. The government, however, established note issuing banks whose notes circulated only in the *départment* in which it was located, and the Banque de France opened branches in a few cities outside Paris from 1836. In the 1840s, a period when there was a prohibition on the establishment of private note issuing banks, the Banque de France established 15 branches between 1841 and 1848. Following the *coup d'état* of 1851, the French government, with the purpose of increasing wealth and improving the economy, encouraged the formation of banks and this led to the creation of joint-stock banks. The government, to reassure the public, also declared that the Banque de France notes were legal tender throughout the country and that there was a limit on the issuing of notes. It thus had an advantage over the private note issuing banks which eventually became part of the Banque de France. By 1900 the Banque de France had branches in the main cities and towns, as well as, other types of offices throughout the country.

Crédit Mobilier, established in 1852 became the model for the *banques mixtes* in Europe. By the 1870s this type of bank, whose aim was to provide capital for industry was inappropriate and inadequate to meet the demands of industry and was surpassed in its aims by the emergence of a government and industrial stock market. Other banks emerged such as Crédit Industriel et Commercial, established in 1859, Crédit Lyonnais, established in 1863 and now merged with Crédit Agricole, and Société Générale, established a year later. The Banque de Paris et des Pays-Bas, a *banque d'affaires*, was founded in 1872, followed by the Banque de l'Union Parisienne, another *banque d'affaires,* in 1904. The effect of the founding of these specialised banks was the strengthening of the financial infrastructure. In 1919 the Crédit National was founded and provided medium and long-term credit for industry, while other banks were encouraged to lend to small and medium sized businesses.[21] From the 1830s to the 1850s French foreign lending was mainly directed to the recently independent Belgium, in the form of purchases of securities. In the 1900s there was renewed interest in Belgium. Indeed, Deutsche Bank opened a branch in Brussels in 1910 to raise funds for German industry, having done likewise in London in 1872.[22]

From the mid 19th century foreign lending was directed to Austria, Italy and Spain. Following the Franco-Prussian War most foreign investment was directed to Russia due to the French government seeking it as an ally and also due to events in Germany, previously a lender to Russia, which was directing whatever capital that was available to the investment in and the development of its indigenous industry. Germany and Russia also engaged in a trade war through tariffs in the 1880s. The restriction in 1887 on German banks lending against Russian state bonds, 60% of which were in German possession, led to a decline in their price.[23] These were purchased by French investors and in turn France became the most important creditor to Russia, though the funds flowed to the former bondholders in Germany.

International finance in France was influenced by trade and diplomacy. It was not the only country that intervened in the direction of international capital flows. Following the cessation of the Sino-Japanese war in 1895 the Hongkong and Shanghai Bank wanted to issue a British loan solely, with British government support, on behalf of China to which it had in recent years been principal banker. The British government which rarely intervened in private matters of banks decided otherwise following advice that the loan should be issued by three countries, the United Kingdom, France and Russia, for diplomatic reasons and also due to the size of the loan. Eventually, however, through a separately negotiated alliance, the loan was issued in Paris and guaranteed by Russia.[24]

Germany finances industrial development

The German Reich, founded in 1870, was relatively late in industrialising. The creation of the Zollverein in 1834 and the construction of railroads are considered the beginnings of industrialisation. Private banks were the most important form of banking up to 1870, although there were universal type banks in existence conducting commercial and investment banking services, such as, the Disconto-Gesselschaft and the Berliner Handel Gesselschaft. The Reichsbank was founded in 1875 and became the successor to the note issuing Prussian Bank and to those in other states that became part of Germany. The direction of whatever German capital was available for export was influenced by government policy.

The German capital market was fragmented with several financial centres in Frankfurt, Hamburg and Cologne, and which were quite separate and provided different banking services. Frankfurt specialised in public finance, Hamburg in trade finance and Cologne in industrial finance.[25] Frankfurt was the most important financial centre until Berlin became the central capital market of the Reich, in particular due to the founding of the *Grössbanken,* universal banks. The universal banks held large direct holdings in German industry and often had seats on the boards of large industrial firms. Berlin never became the leading continental European financial centre as most of the available capital was used for domestic industrial development.

Switzerland's internationally active banks and capital exports

Switzerland's banks were active internationally and the country was a large exporter of capital. The Confederation of Switzerland was created in 1848, which prior to that was an association of cantons. Geneva had always been an international financial center ever since trade fairs were held there and was also the centre of the Huguenot international network, with strong connections to Paris. Jean Necker, from Geneva whose bank was one the largest in Paris in the 1770s, became Comptroller in France in 1776. In 1781, Jean Fréderic Perregaux from Neuchâtel in Switzerland opened a bank in Paris and later became one of the co-founders and early governors of the Banque de France. Hans Konrad Hottinger with Zurich origins also opened a bank in Paris, in 1785, and was one of the most important bankers to the French cotton industry. Isaac Panchaud, another Swiss, established the Caisse d'Escompte, which became part of the Banque de France.[26]

By the early part of the 20th century the Swiss banks had large amounts of foreign investments primarily due to the inflows of foreign capital though they had few foreign branches. While Switzerland became a leading centre for capital inflows due to its neutrality, political stability and banking secrecy, it was also a capital exporter. In 1914, there were only four branches of Swiss banks abroad and this had increased to only six by 1943. They were represented though in the main international financial centres. Crédit Suisse, established in 1856, and the Swiss Bank Corporation, established in 1872, both had branches in New York in 1939. Prior to that Swiss Bank Corporation had opened a branch in London in 1898.

The proportion of investments by large Swiss banks that was foreign investments had reached 55% as early as 1906. This foreign element steadily declined so that by 1913 the proportion was 32% and by 1940 it had declined to 25% of their total investments. By 1913 Switzerland had $2.7 billion in foreign investments, which in per capita terms was more than that of the United Kingdom's. By 1938 its foreign investments were $2.3 billion. There was a large increase by the mid 1940s in its foreign investments, much of which was capital imports reinvested abroad. By the early 1960s foreign claims amounted to 15.8% of Swiss banks' total assets increasing to 38.6% by the early 1970s.[27]

European banking systems and national economies in the 19th century

The banking system in the 19th century was much more developed in the United Kingdom than in the other main European countries. Table 1.1 outlines the ratio of the number of bank offices to total population, that is the density, in the first half of the 19th century. The French banking system was the least developed of these countries and

Table 1.1 Ratio of Bank Offices to Total Population

	Number	Year	Ratio	Number	Year	Ratio
United Kingdom*	447	1801	0.48	1,135	1841	0.71
France	64	1800	0.025	304	1840	0.10
Germany**	320	1820	0.30	439	1849	0.27

* The United Kingdom refers to England and Wales
** Germany refers to Prussia. Private bank and unincorporated bank-like institutions in Prussia.
Source: Cameron, R., Banking in the Early Stages of Industrialisation, Oxford University Press, 1967, Chart II.2, p. 28; Tables IV.2, p. 111; V.1, p. 138; VI.2, p. 161 and text p. 298

by 1840 only had a moderate to low density. There were only four joint stock banks there in 1800, three in Paris and one in the provinces, while there were 60 private banks, 10 in Paris and 50 in the provinces. This explains the very low density in 1800. By 1840 there were only 21 joint stock banks, six of these were in Paris and 15 were in the provinces, and three branches, while the number of private banks increased to 30 in Paris and to 250 in the provinces. In the 1840s there were prohibitions on the establishment of private note issuing banks.

From 1850 onwards there was an increase in joint-stock banks in both Paris and the provinces with a general decline in the number of private banks. By 1870 encouraged by the government, there were 17 joint stock banks in Paris and 132 in the provinces, along with 100 branches, although the number of private banks declined to 20 in Paris and 200 in the provinces.[28]

The proportion of bank assets to national income and national wealth are measures of the size of the banking industry in an economy. The data for bank assets as a proportion of national income and national wealth are outlined in Table 1.2.

The French proportion is the lowest in the mid 19th century although by 1913 it was closer to the United Kingdom's. Indeed, Japan was ahead of France with a proportion of bank assets to national income of 16.1% in the early 1880s, only 10 years after the modernisation of its banking system. There are significant increases in the size of the banking sector in each country, especially in France, Germany and the United States, partly due to their relatively underdeveloped systems in the late 19th century. In France it increased three times, although the increases in the United States and Germany were much larger by 1913. The development of banking in these countries in the period 1875–1913 was much later than in the United

Table 1.2 Bank Assets as a Proportion of National Income and National Wealth

	National Income Percentage	Year	National Income**** Percentage	National Wealth***** Percentage
			1913	1913
United Kingdom*	34.4	1844	54	12
Germany**	31.1	1865	63	14
United States***	29.8	1871	72	16
France	15.6	1870	45	10
Japan	16.1	1878–1882	–	–

* The United Kingdom refers to England and Wales in 1844
** Germany refers to Prussia in 1865
*** The United States' national income in 1871 is a percentage of GNP 1864–1873. National Wealth for the United States refers to 1912
**** 1913 national income is calculated based on Cameron assuming national wealth to be between 4 and 5 times national income.
***** National Wealth is the aggregate of real assets but not financial assets.
Source: Cameron, R., Banking in the Early Stages of Industrialisation, Oxford University Press, 1967, Tables IX.1, p. 302; IX.2, p. 305

Kingdom where there was a system of joint stock banks and country banks, as well as the internationally oriented private bankers and which by that time London was the dominant international financial centre. The French government had commenced in the 1850s to encourage the development of banking, especially in the provinces, whereas Germany as a unified country itself and the *Grössbanken* were only founded in 1870. The United States' banking system at this time was fragmented and the country was a net importer of capital for economic development.

Financial and tangible assets of selected countries at various stages of development in the 19th century are outlined in Table 1.3. The financial interrelations ratio, which is the ratio of financial to tangible assets in a country, is another measure of the development of banking. It compares the relative size of countries' financial superstructures. The ratio in the United States in 1805 was the same as it was in Japan in 1885, and the ratio in France in 1815 was close to that in Germany in 1850. The United States also had almost three times more tangible than financial assets, France more than six times and Germany five and a half times.

In the last quarter of the 18th century and during the 19th century, well into the modern banking era, several events influenced the world order and international banking. These were independence of the United States in 1776, revolution in France in 1789, independence of

Table 1.3 Financial Assets to Tangible Assets Multiples of Gross National Product*

	United States 1805	France 1815	Germany 1850	Japan 1885
Assets				
Tangible	2.3	6.5	9.4	6.3
Financial	0.7	1.0	1.7	1.9
Financial Interrelations Ratio	.30	.14	.18	.30

* Tangible assets are real assets and are the sum of land, agriculture and other, and reproducible tangible assets such as equipment and inventories, livestock and household goods. Financial assets consist of mortgages, trade credit, consumer credit as well as government securities.

Source: Cameron, R., Banking in the Early Stages of Industrialisation, Oxford University Press, 1967, Table 4-3, p. 58

countries in Latin America from the 1810s, the end of the Napoleonic Wars and the continental blockade in 1815 and, the most significant of all in terms of industrial development, the industrial revolution and the innovations in transport and communications. Outside of Europe, the United States was the main industrial country in the late 19th century. The United Kingdom's share of world trade in manufactures declined from the turn of the century up to World War I while those of the United States and Germany were increasing.

Economic data also illustrate the emergence of the United States and Germany. The annual average growth rates of per capita real gross domestic product between 1820 and 1870 were 1.5% in the United States, 1.2% in the United Kingdom and 0.8% in France. In Germany it was 0.7%. In 1870 the United Kingdom was ranked first in terms of gross domestic product per capita, with the United States second, France third, Canada fourth, Germany fifth and Japan sixth. By 1913 the United Kingdom was ranked second behind the United States, and Canada was ranked ahead of France, with the other two countries ranked the same.[29]

The United States and the shift in economic power and the centre of international finance

At the beginning of the 19th century the banking system in the United States was characterised by a large number of small banks without a developed nationwide network. This was partly due to the widespread distrust of the power of large banks. Prior to independence indigenous banks were not permitted. The first chartered bank was the Bank of Philadelphia, in 1780 and which became Bank of North America in 1782. Interstate branching was first developed with the Bank of the United States, modelled on the Bank of England. It was established in Philadelphia for financing the government and to establish national banking and to provide credit. This was chartered for 20 years by Congress in 1791 with the power to issue notes and conduct private and government business. The charter was not renewed due to objections by state banks and a change in the political administration.[30]

In 1816, there were approximately 250 state-chartered banks increasing to 600 by 1836 and to 1,600 by 1863. Between 1811 and 1816 there was no national currency until the Second Bank of the United States was founded to finance war debts and for currency stability. There was opposition to it from other banks due to its advantage in size and its support by the government in providing it with capital. It was also considered as favouring the relatively wealthier eastern states as its regulations disadvantaged banks in the more rural western states. Furthermore, it became a subject of the re-election campaign of the outgoing President, who was of the same opinion and who had the support of the western states. This bank lasted until 1836 when following re-election of the President its charter was not renewed.[31] Both of these banks had many foreigners as shareholders. From 1836 to 1863 banks issued their own notes during what is termed the free banking era.

The National Banking Act of 1864 legislated for the founding of national banks and also the creation of the Office of the Comptroller of the Currency. There was an initial surge in national banks though many state banks did not seek national charters due to the more stringent regulations. By 1913 there were 26,664 national and state chartered banks and 19,197 of these were state chartered, with an average size in assets of less than half of a national bank. A feature of the banking system was unit banking and that branching had not developed. In 1910, 26 of the then 46 states had no branching and only eight states allowed state-wide branching. This had increased to only 18 of the then 48 states with state-wide branching by 1939, with a further 12 states allowing geographically limited branching and 14 states having only unit banking.[32] From the end of the civil war until 1913 when the Federal Reserve Board was founded, in what is termed the national banking era, there was no central bank. The Federal Reserve Act was enacted partly as a reaction to financial difficulties during the gold standard. The United States had returned to the gold standard in 1879 for the first time since the civil war. National banks were obliged to become members of the Federal Reserve System, while state banks were not, and national banks were permitted to establish foreign branches and accept foreign bills of exchange. Prior to this, national banks were prohibited from branching abroad. Edge Act corporations were introduced in 1919 to allow banks, both American and foreign banks with offices in the United States, to establish subsidiaries to provide international banking services in several states, including accepting deposits and making loans, to overcome interstate banking restrictions.

Certain sections of the Banking Act of 1933, known as the Glass-Steagall Act, separated commercial and investment banking services that could be provided by banks. Prior to this there was a universal type banking system in the United States with investment banks frequently having directors on the boards of firms in which it had long-term investments. It was section VIII of the Clayton Act of 1914 which first partially eliminated this element of universal banking by prohibiting directors to be on the boards of different companies in the same industry. This prohibition thus restricted the investment banks' ability to nominate a partner to sit on several boards in the same industry and their ability to source information from several firms in specific industries.[33] The later Glass-Steagall Act had a compounding effect on the long-term financing of industry, whereby banks were replaced by institutional investors. Another effect of the legislation was to protect investment banks from competition from the large commercial banks. They also gained an advantage due to their specialisation and when they went abroad there was no opposition from commercial banks in the other main international financial centre, London.[34] One such investment bank that became one of the bulge bracket Wall Street banks as a consequence of the act was Morgan Stanley, which emerged from J.P. Morgan, a bank specialising in commercial banking although it was in the privileged position of being the only commercial bank that was allowed to transact limited investment banking business. This restriction on the division of banking business has since been relaxed.

Prior to World War I the United States was a net debtor. In 1913 it had borrowed $3.7 billion but by 1919 it had a become a net international creditor of a similar amount, much of this being due to the liquidation of American assets held by the British and borrowing by the United Kingdom to finance the war.[35] In the post World War I period the London based private bankers who were the core of the pre-war international financial system were unable to reconstitute a similar international banking system and network that had existed before.

New York emerged as a leading international financial centre in the 1920s and Europe depended on capital from the United States.

Due to the war European exports to Latin America declined and American investors filled the void. The United Kingdom had been the largest investor in Latin America prior to the war. London bankers withdrew investments there and this allowed the United States to become its largest investor. American investments in Latin America tripled in the 1920s and doubled in Europe and Canada and American banks expanded abroad to exploit these opportunities.[36] By the 1930s, though, there were protectionist policies in place in most countries and the United States was a leading proponent of tariffs, exemplified by the Smoot-Hawley Tariff Act of 1930.

Japan's modernisation and internationalisation

In 1639 Japan restricted international trade to a few trading partners and this policy secluded it from exposure to technological innovations until its reversal towards free trade in the late 1850s. The 1860s was the beginning of rapid industrialisation from an economy of relatively underdeveloped levels of technology and Japan required capital for this purpose, much the same as Germany had for its industrial development, although in a more advanced economy.

The Japanese banking system was late in modernising relative to other countries commencing in the 1870s following the Meiji restoration in 1868. The internationalisation of Japanese banking is a recent phenomenon. The Japanese banking system was based originally on an American model, later replaced by a British model for commercial banking and the French Crédit Mobilier model for investment banking. The model for the Bank of Japan was suggested by Say, the French finance minister, and was based on the National Bank of Belgium as this was considered the most appropriate to Japan's requirements.[37] To counter dependence on foreign banks and to establish a presence in international banking the Japanese government established the Yokohama Specie Bank in 1880 and established branches in London and New York that same year. It also had branches in Paris and Berlin in the 1930s, as well as 32 branches in China and 93 branches in the Straits countries. Its successor, the Bank of Tokyo, which merged in 1996 with Mitsubishi Bank, was the only bank permitted to have foreign branches until the 1970s.[38] Japan was the largest trading country with China from 1890 and much of Japan's foreign investment was directed to China following the Russo-Japanese War in 1905 until the late 1930s. These investments were supported with funds obtained from the postal savings system.[39]

Due to restrictive provisions contained in the National Banks Law of 1872 only four such joint stock banks or ordinary banks were established by 1876 and following amendments to it there were 603 national banks by 1881. Specialised banks were also created for the long-term funding of industry, such as, the Industrial Bank of Japan. Thus at the turn of the 20th century a modern financial system composed of ordinary and savings banks, long-term credit banks, and a stock exchange, founded in 1878, was in place. This was added to by the founding of securities firms in the 1910s and trust companies in the 1920s. By 1900 there were 1,854 ordinary as well as 435 savings banks. This number was reduced to 65, comprising 61 ordinary banks and four savings banks, by 1945. The Savings Bank Law of 1921 and the Banking Law of 1927, as well as mergers promoted by the Ministry of Finance, were the factors for this. From 1949 there were no savings banks and the ordinary banks consisted of city banks and regional banks. The Trust Fund Bureau was the central administrative centre of the Postal Savings Banks and provided much of the capital required for post-war reconstruction.[40]

One of the most important banking regulations introduced during the second era of banking reform was Article 65 of the Securities and Exchange Law of 1947. This ostensibly separated commercial and investment banking and was similar to, but not the same as, the Glass-Steagall provisions in the United States. In fact, there was no provision for total separation of activities and Japanese banks were involved in the securities business through advising on underwriting, purchasing stock on their own account and through affiliations with securities firms.[41]

With the decline of Yokohama as an international financial centre and the Bank of Tokyo superseding the activities of the Yokohama Specie Bank following its dissolution, Tokyo became the leading financial centre and has consolidated this position by becoming one of the leading international financial centres. A study by Reed reveals that in 1900, and also in 1925, Yokohama was ranked higher than Tokyo and that Tokyo only emerged in the 1960s as the leading financial centre along with another important financial centre, Osaka. In 1965 foreign financial assets of banks located in Tokyo amounted to $2.4 billion and this increased to $44 billion in 1978. This was much lower than in London and New York, and also than in Paris or Frankfurt, and most of the claims were in countries in east and south-east Asia.[42] The internationalisation of Japanese banks in the post World War II period is closely correlated with foreign direct investment by Japanese firms. In the 40 years up to 1992 this amounted to $386.5 billion in total with 44% of investment directed to North America, 20% to Europe and 22% to Asia and Oceania.[43]

International financial centres in the late 19th century and early 20th century

International financial centres are *entrepôts* for capital and centres for international payments and settlements clearing. London was the undisputable leading international financial centre in the first half of the 19th century though Paris was also important in continental Europe in the late 19th century. In 1914 French banks had most of their foreign investment in Europe, whereas British banks had only a minority. None of the three financial centres in Germany ever gained the same international status as London or Paris. For a while in the inter-war period New York became the hegemonic international financial centre, commensurate with its country's status in international relations. Thereafter there have been synchronous financial centres sharing the hegemony.

The United Kingdom was on the gold standard since 1821 when silver's status as legal tender was discontinued for transactions, having been earlier discontinued for those transactions over £25 in 1774.[44] This factor along with the stability of sterling and the confidence in its convertibility into gold, the role of sterling and that of the sterling bill in international trade and in finance, the system of specialised services of accepting and discounting of bills, and the availability of capital for investment abroad, contributed to London maintaining its status as the leading international financial centre, once it had attained it, until World War I. International communications were also a factor. Telegraphic communications were introduced between London and Paris in 1852 and between London and New York in 1866, the source of the term 'cable' used to describe the dollar–pound exchange rate. Australia and the East, including Japan, were linked in the 1870s.

The availability of credit and its external flow was an important factor in the support of the gold standard and a factor in sustaining *Pax Britannica*. The international financial system of this period could be considered a credit system managed by private banks based in London.[45] Between 1880 and 1900 the number of banks in the United Kingdom declined from 385 to 259, due to mergers and acquisitions.

However, the number of British, colonial and foreign banks that had offices or agencies, most of which were located in London, increased from 102 to 988.[46] The importance of London as an international financial centre, more so than Paris or Berlin, is illustrated by the balance sheet total of banks. The aggregate balance sheet total in 1914 for banks with head offices in London was £1,069 million, in Paris £404.2 million and in Berlin £304.3 million.[47]

Another factor in London gaining its status as the leading international financial centre in 19th century was the influence of its national economy in the global economy, although a significant characteristic of London was that it continued to maintain this status though the United Kingdom economy was in relative decline from the last quarter of the 19th century and during the inter-war period. The international financial centre had essentially decoupled from the national economy.[48] The political influence of continental European governments on the direction of foreign investment was an advantage for London over other European centres. French capital exports were often dependent on corresponding exports of French products.

Where London triumphed over Paris was its ability to raise capital for lending abroad, additionally supplied by the country banks' surpluses and its trade surpluses. The Franco-Prussian war, the subsequent leaving of the gold standard and the bi-metallic system of payment, continued even after the Latin Monetary Union, of which it was a member, moved to gold only, also contributed to the dominance of London, although there was some resurgence in Paris in the 1890s largely due to lending to Russia. Table 1.4 outlines some foreign deposits in London, Paris and Berlin in 1913. British Empire deposits were the largest single component in London while Russian deposits were the largest in Paris, placed there to encourage investment in Russian bonds although the government was also actively promoting the purchase of these bonds.

Between 1921 and 1924 there were similar amounts of new issues in New York and London, $2,373 million and $2,470 million respectively. This was insufficient to meet even the demands for war reparations and reconstruction alone. Between 1924 and 1929 New York raised $6.4 billion in foreign investment and London almost half this amount, $3.3 billion.[49] Total new issues in New York between 1920 and 1931 amounted to $9.4 billion. The equivalent amount for new issues in London was $6.3 million. British Empire issues were almost the same in New York and London, $2.1 billion and $2.4 billion, respectively. This was largely due to Canada preferring the New York

Table 1.4 Foreign Deposits in London, Paris and Berlin 1913
US Dollar Millions

London		Paris		Berlin	
Origin	**Amount**	**Origin**	**Amount**	**Origin**	**Amount**
British possessions	150.0	Russian Government	221.8	Russian Monetary Authority	53.0
Japanese Government and Bank of Japan	101.7	Bank of Greece	19.0	Chile	34.8
Yokohama Specie Bank	80.8	Bank of Japan	13.0	Italian Bank of Issue	17.8
Bank of Russia	23.7	Italian Treasury	7.5	Sweden	15.4
Reichsbank	14.0	Reichsbank	5.4	National Bank of Panama	10.5
National Bank of Greece	10.0			Bank of Austro-Hungary	8.3
Other European Banks	63.0				

Source: de Cecco, M., Money and Empire: The International Gold Standard, 1890–1914, Blackwell, Oxford, 1974, pp. 105–108

market. Issues by foreign firms were a larger amount in London, $2.4 billion, almost 40% of the total issues, though they were relatively unimportant in New York, $1.9 billion, 20% of the total issues. Firms had switched to obtaining finance directly from banks.[50]

During World War I the United Kingdom was a borrower in New York. In the three years from the beginning of the war it borrowed $1,250 million, the largest single borrower and with almost twice the borrowings of France. Russia and Germany also borrowed but these amounts were relatively insignificant. Investments to the value of $3 billion, previously held by Europeans, were also re-sold to American investors. When the United States entered the war in 1917 it was mostly financed through the sale of Treasury bonds, raising $21.5 billion in two years.[51] The sale of securities by American bankers to individuals was to continue in the 1920s with the individual investor becoming an important target and source of funds.

In the post World War I period the United Kingdom was weakened and the London-based private bankers who were at the core of international banking withdrew from many foreign markets, especially in Latin America, where previously they were dominant as was British foreign direct investment. The return to the gold exchange standard by the United Kingdom in 1925 at the pre-war rate affected the competitiveness of its exports and, along with a reduction in the amount of capital available and in current account surpluses, foreign bond issues moved to New York. Foreign issues were not possible in continental European markets until 1924. The gold exchange standard was reinstated when other countries returned to it between 1925 and 1926 but it was to last only until 1931. France's position was also weakened by the war and their investments in Russia were worthless after the revolution in 1917. Germany was disadvantaged by war reparations and by 1924 had become a net debtor with spiralling inflation rates.

New York emerged as the leading international financial centre only when the pre-war London based network of private international bankers was unable to continue their pre-war system, and also due to the pressure on the pound in the crisis of 1931, the subsequent liquidity crisis and inconvertibility of sterling and the introduction of exchange controls.[52]

The United Kingdom had balance of payments deficits for most of this period while the United States had payments surpluses throughout most of the 1920s. Throughout the 1920s there were large capital outflows from the United States, mostly consisting of new foreign bond issues in New York. American banks began to operate more actively in international markets encouraging investors to invest in these.[53]

Some of the reasons that the United States' balance of payments surpluses and its international lending were not more closely linked were due to the domestic demand for capital, the relatively small share of international trade in its gross national product and the relatively internationally less developed American investment banks.[54] In addition, American investors' preferences were for equities over foreign bonds and the Federal Reserve Board was more interested in domestic rather than international affairs.[55]

Despite the emergence of New York as the leading international financial centre, foreign bond issues in New York peaked in 1927 at only 18% of the total securities issues and they had declined to 7% of the total by 1929.[56] This was due to interest rate increases in 1928 which had the effect of increasing demand for domestic securities. In the second half of 1928 foreign lending was zero.[57] The inter-war hegemony of New York, due more to London's lack of capital and the United Kingdom's financial difficulties than its own international dimension, would be challenged in the post World War II period.

From the 1860s European governments, public authorities and firms had financed themselves by means of direct financing, that is, selling bonds or securities to the public through banks. This period of what is termed 'security capitalism' continued until the outbreak of the World War I and existed for a while in the 1920s. During the inter-war period it was replaced by indirect financing through intermediaries.[58]

The internationalisation of banks from the 19th century to the mid 20th century

Much of the internationalisation of banking was due to the expansion of private bankers abroad and creating networks for the flow of capital and information. Merchant banks in the 19th century were involved in financing international trade and issuing foreign bonds, though this international business was conducted without hardly any foreign branches. Most of the merchant banks in London had been founded by foreigners, many of whom were attracted there due to its importance in trade. Many of these bankers were in other industries before becoming bankers. From Germany came Baring, Johann Baring initially commencing as a draper in Exeter, and Rothschild, Nathan Rothschild originally being in cotton trading in Manchester before establishing a branch of the family's bank.[59]

Also from Germany were Schroder, later to become part of Salomon, Smith Barney and now part of Citigroup, Kleinworth, later Kleinworth Benson and then part of Dresdner Bank and now part of Allianz, and Warburg, which was acquired by Swiss Bank Corporation and which later merged with Union Bank of Switzerland to become United Bank of Switzerland. Hambro, came from Denmark though the family originated in Hamburg, and the bank is now part of Société Générale while Lazard, with French origins, came via the United States. Baring and Company, now part of ING Bank, along with Hope and Company, from Rotterdam, later Mees and Hope, then MeesPierson, and now part of Fortis, were the leading bankers to European governments until overtaken by Rothschilds in the 1820s, which became the leading bank in the world in the mid 19th century. Rothschilds was created in 1810 as M.A. Rothschild and Söhne, in Frankfurt, specialising in large scale international lending and payments with family members establishing banks in London and Paris as well as branches in other European cities. Bethmann was an important German bank based in Frankfurt. In 1788 it was quite innovative in raising capital from the public's savings to finance a state loan issuing what were termed Bethmann bonds.[60]

The strong link between trade and banking was instrumental in the rise in the 18th century of Hope and Company which like many other firms migrated into banking. It moved to London in 1795 during the French occupation of the United Provinces. Barings was the agent for the American government and in 1803, along with Hope and Company, arranged a loan, issued in Amsterdam, of $11 million for the purchase of Louisiana from France. Barings alone was the most important lender to the American government up to the mid 19th century.

With the spread of technology, the development of heavy industry and the onset of railway construction many bankers found it difficult to raise the large sums of capital required to finance these industries. Considering the long-term maturity of such loans a more effective form of banking was required. Joint-stock banking developed. The first joint-stock investment bank was the Société Générale pour le Dévelopment du Commerce et de l'Industrie founded in Belgium in 1822. The first private joint stock banks established in the United Kingdom were in 1826. Crédit Mobilier was founded in France in 1852 by the Perreires and became the model for universal banking in Europe. It had many subsidiaries abroad. In the United Kingdom it operated as the International Finance Society, as well as having subsidiaries in Spain, operating as Credito Mobilario Espanol, in Germany operating as Damstadter Bank, in Italy as Credito Mobiliare Italiano and in the Netherlands as Crédit Néerlandais.

Private merchant banks continued to develop and were the most important international bankers in London by the late 19th century and were to the forefront in the development of London as an international financial centre. In 1890 the most important of these London bankers in terms of partners' capital and shareholders' funds were, Rothschilds, £6.7 million, Barings, £2.9 million, J.S. Morgan, £1.8 million, Seligmans, £1.5 million, Lazards, £1.2 million, Schroders, £1.1 million, Hambros, £1.0 million with Kleinworth, £0.8 million. In fact, most of these independent merchant banks founded during the 19th century were practically the same until the 1990s.[61]

British overseas banks began to establish in the 1830s. Between 1830 and 1914, 70 British overseas banks were founded. The most important were the Standard Bank of British South Africa, now part of Standard Chartered Bank, and the London and River Plate Bank both established in 1862 and the Hongkong and Shanghai Banking Corporation established in 1865.[62] Another was Grindlays Bank, now part of the ANZ Banking Group. By 1890 there were 32 British owned and registered overseas banks with 711 foreign branches. Thereafter the number of banks declined and by 1985 there were only five overseas banks with 1,016 branches. However, many banks were locally registered from the 1950s and when these are added to the British registered overseas banks then the total number of banks in 1985 was 55 with 4,990 branches. At the turn of the century and throughout the first half of the 20th century Australasia was the most important location for their foreign operations with 32 overseas banks having 444 branches there. Even though there were only 13 British overseas banks by 1970, the number of branches had continued to increase in this region to 1,767. Southern Africa was the second most important location for the overseas banks with the number of branches there peaking at 1,281 in 1955, representing 17 overseas banks. They were prominent in the North America up to 1913 where there were 103 branches of 28 overseas banks, rapidly declining to 24 overseas banks with four branches by 1928. Most of these overseas banks were involved in trade finance and in domestic banking in the locations where they were established.[63] The Deutsche Ubersee-Bank, later the Deutche Uberseeische Bank, was founded by Deutsche Bank. It had strong links with Latin America, especially, Argentina.[64] In the early 20th century Société Générale de Belgiue, now part of Fortis Bank, established the Banque Sino-Belge for business with China and the Banque Brésilienne Italo-Belge for business in Latin America. Likewise other European banks created overseas business, either alone or as part of a consortium. A consortium of banks consisting of among others Deutsche Bank and Basler Bankverein, later becoming Swiss Bank Corporation through mergers, founded Banca Commerciale in Milan in 1894. Swiss Bank Corporation, as it was then, was one of the founding banks of Banque Internationale de Bruxelles in 1898. Crédit Suisse founded an overseas bank, the Schweizerische-Argentinische Bank in 1910 becoming part of Schweizerische-Sudamericanische Bank in 1912 as a parent bank for the former with its head office in Zurich and branches in Buenos Aires and Lugano.[65] Of course, many banks also had share holding in foreign banks and some were represented on the board. The French government established five overseas banks in the 1850s each designated to specific colonial regions.[66]

American banks were only allowed to establish abroad following the Federal Reserve Act in 1913. Citibank opened a branch in Buenos Aires in 1914 and in the 1920s it and other banks began to expand in Latin America as British banks began to divest from there in the post World War I period and also due to the large increase in trade between that region and the United States and to follow the increased investment there by American firms.

By 1930 Citibank, now part of Citigroup, had 97 foreign branches with about two-thirds in Latin America. There were eight Federal Reserve System banks in 1960 that had foreign offices. Citibank and Chase Manhattan Bank, later acquired by Chemical Bank in 1996 though retaining the Chase brand and now part of JPMorgan Chase, dominated with wholly owned offices in 20 and 11 countries respectively.[67] American banks focused in particular on American firms in Europe and they were also approaching European firms with better terms and the most active of these were Citibank, Morgan Guaranty Trust, Bank of America and Chase Manhattan Bank.[68]

Consortium banks

In the 1960s and 1970s several international bank groups were formed as consortium banks to participate in international lending and the Euromarkets. The main reasons for their emergence and upsurge were due to American banks' competition, the management and sharing of risk in international lending and the scarcity of personnel, particularly for the increasingly important euromarkets. Consortia require only a moderate amount of investment, and correspondingly control, for a single member bank and require few personnel.

Midland and International Banks Limited, established in 1964, is considered the first of the consortium banks and was comprised of Midland Bank, Toronto Dominion Bank, the Commercial Bank of Australia and, the mainly African centred, Standard Bank later to merge with the Chartered Bank of India and now part of Standard Chartered Bank. It was established as part of Midland Bank's desire to have closer links with Commonwealth banks and to share knowledge and information in medium and long-term financing.[69] Commerzbank, the Westminster Bank, later, National Westminster Bank, formed through a merger of the National Provincial Bank and the Westminster Bank and now part of the Royal Bank of Scotland, First National Bank of Chicago, the Irving Trust Company of New York and the Hongkong and Shanghai Banking Corporation, HSBC, founded the International Commercial Bank in 1967 to provide long-term financing. In the same year Dresdner Bank, Bank of America, Barclays Bank, Banque National de Paris, formed through a merger of

Comptoir National d'Escompte de Paris and Banque Nationale pour le Commerce et l'Industrie, Algemene Bank Nederland, now part of ABN AMRO, and Banca Nazionale del Lavoro established the Société Financière Européenne based in Paris and Luxembourg with the purpose of financing industry. The following year Deutsche Bank, Amsterdam-Rotterdam Bank, now part of ABN AMRO, Midland Bank, now part of HSBC, Société Générale de Banque, Société Générale and Creditanstalt Bankverein of Vienna formed the European-American Bank and Trust Company and the European-American Banking Corporation. Commerzbank, Crédit Lyonnais, now merged with Crédit Agricole, and Banco di Roma established what was termed the Club of Three in 1970. Chase Manhattan Bank, now part of JPMorgan Chase, the National Westminster Bank, the Royal Bank of Canada, and the WestDeutsche Landesbank Girozentrale established the Orion Group in 1971 and established joint subsidiary banks in London, Amsterdam and Hong Kong.[70]

Lloyds Bank, now Lloyds-TSB, Barclays, Barclays DCO, Dominion, Colonial and Overseas, the Australia and New Zealand Bank, the National Bank of New Zealand, BOLSA, the Bank of London and South America, a British overseas bank operating in South America, and the Chartered Bank, established the consortium bank, International Banking Services. Soon after its founding, sterling was devalued in 1967, and loans were restricted even among the member banks to the consortium. Lending in sterling discontinued and the consortium focused mainly on eurocurrency lending. In 1970 the member banks considered that any further expansion of activities by the consortium would be in direct competition with themselves and they also considered that much of the information that was being supplied by the consortium was already widely available to the individual member banks. It was finally dissolved in 1976.[71] The International Joint Bank comprised Sanwa Bank, Mitsui Bank, since merged with Sumitomo Bank, and Kangyo Bank, part of Mizuho Bank, and Nomura Securities. The Japan International Investment Bank consisted of Fuji Bank, also part of Mizuho Bank, Mitsubishi Bank, later merged with the Bank of Tokyo, Sumitomo Bank and Tokai Bank, as well as, Daiwa Securities, Nikko Securities and Yamaichi Securities. These Japanese consortium banks were authorised by the Ministry of Finance in 1970 and the purpose was that the banks and securities firms in the respective consortia would operate in London in the euromarkets to obtain capital for the financing of the internationalisation of Japanese firms.[72]

Many of these consortia did not last very long and those that did were as a result of strong leadership and determination on the part of one of more of the banks in the consortium. The number of consortium banks peaked in 1976. In 1974, a German bank, I.D. Herstatt, became insolvent due to dealings in the foreign exchange market, affecting many of its counterparty banks. The following year, reacting to the bank's activities, the Basle Concordat was issued concerning the supervision of foreign offices. The outcome for banking was that the owning bank and its home central bank were responsible for the solvency of foreign branches, while subsidiaries were the responsibility of the host country regulatory authority. As a result, the regulatory authorities additionally sought guarantees from banks in these consortia. Some merchant banks decided to leave these consortia due to possible liabilities and the size of their balance sheets relative to the larger commercial banks.[73] Many of the consortium banks also discontinued due to the lender of last resort facility not being extended to them.[74]

The onset of contemporary banking

Until World War I European countries were the main foreign investors while the United States was a net debtor, as outlined in Table 1.5. The United Kingdom, France and Germany and, to a lesser although significant extent, Belgium, the Netherlands and Switzerland were the main capital exporters.

The United Kingdom far outpaced the other main creditor countries in terms of volume. From the mid 19th century most of its investments were in projects sponsored by governments in the importing capital country, such as railroad construction and in the provision of public utilities. One of the most important British merchant banks, Barings, was in a crisis in 1890 when they were unable to sell securities on loans granted to Uruguay and Argentina. The Bank of England and other banks assisted them, thus avoiding a run on the banking system. It was rare for the Bank of England to intervene like this but London was the centre of bill accepting and discounting and Barings was a leading acceptance house. Following this it converted its status to that of a limited company. Many other banks were in similar circumstances, affected by the outbreak of war in 1914, as they had lent heavily to German industry during its rapid industrialisation in the pre-war period.

The United States became a foreign investor and Germany a net debtor in the 1920s. During the First World War, European and Latin American countries floated bonds in New York and transformed the United States into a net international creditor.

There was a decline in the volume of international banking during the inter-war period, especially with the unravelling of the gold stan-

Table 1.5 Net Foreign Private Long Term Assets 1855–1913
US Dollar Billions end year

	1855	1870	1885	1900	1913
United Kingdom	1.0	3.5	7.6	12.3	20.4
France	0.5	2.4	3.5	5.0	8.7
Germany	–	–	1.8	3.6	5.5
United States	–0.4	–1.3	–1.8	–2.5	–3.7*

*1914
Source: Fishlow, A., in Van der Wee, H. and Aerts, E. (eds), Debates and Controversies In Economic History, Presses Universitaire de Louvain, 1990, p. 153

dard in the 1930s when sterling became inconvertible in 1931 and the dollar abandoned convertibility in 1933. Protectionism and currency devaluations were the economic policies followed by governments. In terms of capital invested abroad there was not much difference in the total between 1914 and 1938. Table 1.6 outlines the capital invested abroad in these years. France and, particularly, Germany declined in the volume of capital invested abroad in the inter-war period and the United States increased its volume significantly. The total capital invested abroad for these selected countries declined by 8%.

The immediate post World War II period of reconstruction in Europe was assisted by the flow of capital from the United States, initially in the form of Marshall Plan funds from 1947 and thereafter from the mid 1950s through American firms investing directly. The United Kingdom attempted convertibility in 1947 at a rate of $4.03, on the insistence of the United States as part of the conditions of a loan. It was to last six weeks. Devaluation of sterling eventually came in 1949 at the rate of $2.80.

Table 1.6 Gross Nominal Value of Capital Invested Abroad 1914–1938
US Dollar Millions at current exchange rates

	1914	1938
United Kingdom	18,311	17,335
France	8,647	3,859
Germany	5,598	676
United States	3,514	11,491
Total Selected Countries	36,070	33,361

Source: Madisson, A., The World Economy: A Millennial Perspective, Organisation for Economic Growth and Development, Paris, 2001, Tables 2–26a and 2–26b, p. 99

The volumes of accumulated foreign direct investment between 1938 and 1960, as outlined in Table 1.7, illustrate the emergence of the United States as a leading foreign investor. The dominance of foreign direct investment by American firms in the 1950s is evident. Their investments increased fourfold and the share of the total almost doubled. It was a pattern that was to continue throughout the last quarter of the 20th century, although Japanese firms also increased their level of foreign direct investment later during this period, along with German firms. British firms maintained their levels but their share of total foreign direct investment declined significantly from dominating in 1938 with an almost 40% share to 16% in 1960. The amount of foreign direct investment by British firms increased threefold by the late 1970s but their share of the total was lower than in 1960. Significantly American and British firms' share of total foreign direct investment was 67.5% in 1938 and practically the same at 66.1% in 1960, although the vast majority of that was now by American firms.

The era of *Pax Americana* had arrived and the United States was to become the hegemonic country in international relations in the second half of the 20th century. Convertibility of European currencies eventually commenced in 1958, although the Swiss Franc was convertible prior to this. There was a marked decline in the volume of international banking in the inter-war period. Essentially, international banking was conducted on a limited scale between the 1920s and the late 1940s. Banking systems and structures were much the same in the 1950s as they had been twenty years before. All was to change though, with the catalysts for the new banking landscape in

Table 1.7 Estimated Stock of Accumulated Foreign Direct Investment 1938–1960
US Dollar Billions

	1938	Percentage of total	1960	Percentage of total
United Kingdom	10.5	39.8	10.8	16.4
United States	7.3	27.7	32.8	49.7
France	2.5	9.5	4.1	6.2
Japan	0.8	3.0	0.5	0.7
Germany	0.4	1.4	0.8	1.2
Total Selected Countries	21.5	81.4	49.0	74.2
Total Developed Countries	26.4	100	66.0	100

Source: Casson, M., The Growth of International Business, Allen and Unwin, London, 1983, p. 87

the contemporary banking era being the euromarkets, private capital movements and petrodollar recycling, innovations in products and processes and the closer integration of capital markets, floating exchange rates, deregulation and re-regulation, such as co-ordinated international capital adequacy regulations, and the expansion of banks abroad, especially American and Japanese banks.

Part II

The Characteristics of and Influences on Contemporary International Banking

2
Contemporary International Banking Markets

In the post World War II period there were enormous changes in the volume and pattern of world trade and the structure of the world economy. The Bretton Woods Agreement of 1944 ushered in a period of fixed exchange rates. This system was later dismantled in the 1970s with the floating of exchange rates. Exchange controls were also relaxed.

There was resurgence in trade and an increase in the volume of international portfolio investment and foreign direct investment, relative to the tariff driven, protectionist inter-war period. The introduction of commercial satellite in 1965 and the subsequent communications technologies transformed the global economy, as had the telegraph a century earlier. The relatively lower cost of communications and transport has linked time zones and technology has made information easily accessible and its diffusion rapid. American firms had established themselves throughout the world. Japan became a leading creditor country.

In 1899 the United Kingdom had a 34% share of world trade in manufactures, while Germany had a 23% share and the United States 11.5%. By 1913 the United Kingdom's share declined to 31%, while Germany's share increased to 27.5% as did the United States' share to 13%.[1] The United Kingdom's share of world exports of manufactures was 25% in 1950 and had declined to 9% by 1973.[2] From 1870 to 1989 Japan had the highest growth rates of per capita real gross domestic product of the main industrial countries, 2.7% compared to 2% in Germany, 1.9% in the United States, 1.8% in France and 1.4% in the United Kingdom. Between 1950 and 1973 it was 8% compared to 4.9% in Germany, 4% in France, 2.5% in the United Kingdom and 2.2% in the United States. Since the oil crisis of 1973 until 1989 Japan was still ahead of the others with its growth rates at 3.1% compared to 2.1% in Germany, 1.8% in France, the same as in the United Kingdom and 1.6% in the United States.[3]

The Triad emerged and the links to the colonies, that were an integral part of certain European countries economic and political policies for well over a century, were, if not severed, certainly diluted with the 'wind of change' of independence. The European Union was established in 1958, originally as the European Economic Community. Other free trade areas outside of Europe were also established, in particular, the North American Free Trade Agreement between the United States, Canada and Mexico in 1994. The World Trade Organisation, with its increased importance, and that of services, in its negotiations, has contributed to a reduction in trade barriers and a liberalisation of trade. The General Agreement on Trade in Services a derivation of the Uruguay Round of the General Agreement on Tariffs and Trade, had a separate agreement for and annex on financial services.

International banking in London was in the doldrums in the 1950s to such an extent that Morgan Guaranty allowed the lease on its premises on one of the more desirable streets to lapse.[4] London eventually re-emerged as one of the leading international financial centres, although this was based on the euromarkets, which were offshore. British merchant banks, commercial banks and overseas banks, especially the Bank of London and South America, were the main protagonists in this development along with London branches of foreign banks who were later to dominate the euromarkets, as the commercial banks focused on retail lending and the merchant banks, whose balance sheets were insufficient for such business, focused on their core business of corporate finance.[5]

European and American commercial banks had significantly more capital and this ensured that their investment banking divisions had a competitive advantage over the British merchant banks and also over the American investment banks, many of which were private partnerships until recently. The bought deal introduced in the 1980s, whereby a bank, or a few banks, bought a complete issue required a large amount of capital and this also mitigated against them.[6] Those banks that were to the forefront in the promotion of the market in the early years became disadvantaged as it developed. The role of the Bank of England was important in the emergence of the euromarkets in London as it encouraged the banks to develop this type of business and acted in an almost passive manner by allowing the market to develop with minimal regulation. There were also other factors which were in its favour, such as, favourable taxation and available skilled personnel, as well as, the regulations introduced on foreign banking business in the United States.[7]

It was only from the early 1960s that many American banks established abroad to source funds and circumvent regulations such as Regulation Q, which limited banks' interest rates, and the Interest Equalisation Tax of 1963, which was a tax on the interest on foreign bonds purchased by Americans. Foreign branches were also exempted from regulations on the funding of foreign direct investment by American firms. In 1960 only eight banks in the Federal Reserve System had foreign offices, comprising 131 branches and two subsidiaries. Two other initiatives to prevent capital outflows, the foreign direct investment program and the foreign credit restraint program had the effect of increasing the number of American Banks establishing offices abroad from the mid 1960s to the early 1970s. The number of banks with foreign offices increased to 79 in 1970 and to 159 by 1980. By the late 1980s, 155 banks had 902 foreign branches and 860 foreign subsidiaries. Having established networks American Banks then focused on broadening their business. Japanese banks only began expanding abroad from the 1970s especially in the United States and the United Kingdom. The growth rate of assets in foreign branches in the 1980s was much higher than the growth rate of assets in Japan. By 1981 the total amount of assets of Japanese banks in foreign offices was $233 billion with 57% in United Kingdom offices and 32% in United States offices. By the late 1980s the total was $1,120 billion with the respective country shares at 40% and 27%, illustrating the increasing significance of other countries for their foreign direct investment. Japanese banks dominated international banking when ranked by size of assets in the 1980s and part of the 1990s.[8]

Contemporary international banking has its origins in the reconstruction of the global trading economy in the 1950s. There are two distinct sub-periods, that is, the Bretton Woods period up to 1973 and the period of floating exchange rates since then. There are also significant differences in the sources of long-term capital movements. During the Bretton Woods period public long-term capital movements dominated in the early 1950s and were practically the same volume as private long-term capital flows up to the early 1970s. Thereafter private long-term capital flows dominate. This banking era is characterised, in particular, by innovations in markets, products and processes, and the rapid diffusion of these innovations has been a catalyst for the globalisation of financial markets. Technology has assisted in the development and implementation of innovations although the network of banks' foreign offices facilitated their diffusion. The difficulty in patenting financial innovations and the mobility of personnel between banks has contributed to the short time lag between the implementation, the imitation and their widespread application of innovations.

International money and capital markets

The international money markets comprise international bank deposits and lending, as well as, eurocurrency deposits and lending. The international capital market is composed of the foreign bond market and the eurobond market. These international markets are both national and supranational. The onshore international money and capital markets consist of banks' foreign transactions with customers in various national markets and the issuing of foreign bonds. The offshore supranational money and capital markets consist of the euromarkets. This is illustrated in Figure 2.1.

Euromarkets consist of the eurocurrency market, part of the international money market, and the eurobond market, part of the international capital market, both providing access to unregulated funds on a large scale.

The eurocurrency market is a supranational market for money in currencies held outside the country of origin of the currency. Deposits consist of time deposits and certificates of deposit. Lending consists of syndicated lending, and euronotes, that is, commercial paper and medium-term notes.

The eurobond market is a supranational market in bonds issued in a eurocurrency and held outside of the country of the currency of issue of the bond. Eurobonds are bonds issued by residents and non-residents in a foreign currency. Therefore, location of issue, currency of issue and residency of issuer are the criteria for determining the status of a bond. However, the definition does not include the residency of the investor. According to the Bank for International Settlements bonds issued in a domestic currency may be classified as eurobonds when the issuer is either resident or non-resident and the investor is

	International Money Market	International Capital Market
Onshore National	International Bank Deposits and Loans	Foreign Bonds
Offshore Supranational	Eurocurrency Deposits and Loans	Eurobonds

Figure 2.1 International Money and Capital Markets

non-resident. They are classified as foreign bonds when the issuer is non-resident and the investor is resident.[9]

Foreign bonds are bonds issued and underwritten by banks on behalf of a foreign borrower in a domestic market and in the currency of the issuing market. The main differences between eurobonds and foreign bonds are that eurobonds are in bearer form and traded over-the-counter whereas foreign bonds may be either in bearer form or registered and traded over-the-counter or on a local exchange. The composition of the issuing syndicate is usually international for eurobond issues and it is mostly domestic banks, or in some instances subsidiaries of foreign banks, for foreign bond issues.

The euromarkets

The euromarkets began to emerge in the late 1950s and the early 1960s. The influx of dollars from Marshall Plan aid, initially, followed by the United States' balance of payments deficits through most of the 1950s, capital movements through military expenditure, foreign investments by Americans to earn higher rates of interest, and the increase in international trade led to an increase in the amount of dollars in Europe.

Regulations in the United States also promoted the development of the Euromarkets along with significant events in the United Kingdom. Regulation Q in the United States prevented banks from offering interest rates above a certain level. At this time there were tight credit controls in Europe and many firms were unable to obtain credit. Exchange controls which had been introduced in 1939 in the United Kingdom as a wartime device were still in place, until they were relaxed in 1979. London recommenced as a centre for clearing in sterling in 1951, though by 1957, the Bank of England restricted this function by banks due to a sterling crisis and pressure on their reserves. The banks continued to clear in dollars.[10] The United Kingdom also introduced restrictions on the lending of sterling to non-residents in 1957, though there were no restrictions on banks lending in foreign currencies. The scene was set.

When the Soviet Union and other countries in the Soviet bloc wanted to hold funds in dollars to pay for future imports they feared confiscation if placed in an American bank. They wanted to keep their foreign earnings in dollars because it was more stable than European currencies and because the rouble was not convertible. They found British banks willing to accept dollar deposits at rates similar to those offered by American banks. Most of the Soviet Union's external financial transactions were directed through the Moscow Narodny Bank in London and the Banque Commerciale pour l'Europe du Nord in Paris. The cable address for the Paris bank was 'eurobank' and hence the origins of the title of the market.

The Bank of England encouraged banks to lend their large surpluses of dollars deposits and the system began to emerge. The dollar was the main trading currency and firms held dollar trading surpluses in dollars rather than convert them into local currencies and also began to borrow dollars in London. These funds were re-deposited in dollars again mostly in banks in London. Once the market developed it became self-sustaining. The market was unregulated and banks could avoid reserve requirements. The euro-dollar currency market became the international money market for lending outside the United States. These developments were accommodated by the Bank of England as they encouraged and further promoted the international attributes of London. With the increase in international trade and the demand for foreign currencies, especially the dollar and to some extent sterling, along with volatile exchange rates since their floating in 1973, it was more beneficial for large internationally trading firms to hold deposits in the currencies of their trading partners instead of converting currencies for international transactions.

What commenced in dollars expanded to other currencies, such that, there are dollar denominated products and also products denominated in other currencies. The market became the eurocurrency market when other currencies were included. Thus the money market part of the euromarkets, the eurocurrency market, a short-term deposit and credit market, mostly inter-bank, and a medium-term market in syndicated loans and euronotes developed. The other part of the market, the eurobond market, a long-term capital market, was soon to emerge due to the existence of its money market counterpart and also due to external factors.

A group of bankers representing Barings, Samuel Montagu, Warburgs and the Bank of London and South America, later to be joined by Hambros, began planning for the re-emergence of London as a leading international capital market. The foreign bond market in New York was increasingly becoming restrictive due to the American balance of payments deficits. At the time there was approximately three billion in dollars outside the United States.[11]

The outflow of dollars, especially to Europe, initiated a regulatory reaction in the United States commencing with a tax on foreign borrowing in the United States' capital market. The Interest Equalisation Tax enacted in 1963, and which came into effect the following year, essentially meant that foreign bonds would have to be discounted before being floated on the New York market. There was approximately a 1% differential between American and European interest rates and the tax was meant to reduce this. It was a tax on the interest on foreign bonds, excluding those of Canada, developing countries and public authorities, which were purchased by American residents. This effectively closed the dollar foreign bond market there. Foreign firms began to borrow dollars from banks instead of issuing bonds in New York leading to a large outflow of dollars. The United States reacted in 1965 by amending the regulation to include loans of one year maturity or more and by introducing voluntary credit restraints on the purchase of foreign securities and foreign lending by American banks. The Interest Equalisation Tax, initially introduced for two years and which was also later increased, was finally abolished in 1974.[12] The effect was similar to that of Regulation Q on the eurocurrency market, accelerating the development of the emerging eurobond market and centering it in London. The first eurobond issue is considered to be Autostrade's, the Italian Motorways Authority, $15 million bearer bond, free from withholding tax, listed in London and Luxembourg in 1963, and lead managed by S.G. Warburg. Other banks in the syndicate were Banque de Bruxelles, Deutsche Bank, and Rotterdamsche Bank.

A few weeks prior to that was the first foreign currency loan in London since World War II when an issue of $20 million on behalf of the Belgian government was organised by Samuel Montagu along with other banks including Schroders and Kleinworth. This is not considered the first eurobond as it was purchased by the participating banks using their eurodollars and there was no retail element.[13]

In 1968, the Office of Foreign Direct Investments was established in the United States and Foreign Direct Investment Rules instigated that American firms had to finance foreign investments above certain levels by borrowing outside the United States to restrain capital flows. This led to increased demand for capital outside the United States and provided further impetus to the eurobond market. This requirement was also discontinued in 1974. With the abolishment of the Interest Equalisation Tax the New York market for foreign bond issues increased rapidly in volume in the 1970s. Similarly in 1965, the then West German government introduced a tax on interest earned by non-residents on fixed income securities effectively diminishing the competition from Frankfurt.

Many American banks established offices in London in the mid 1960s. Their main customers were American firms seeking a means of raising dollars and circumventing their country's regulations. The American investment banks differed from American commercial banks in the type of services they provided for the American firms. The investment banks were providing specialist banking services for the head offices of the firms whereas the commercial banks were providing a range of commercial banking services for the firms' subsidiaries.[14]

There were 98 foreign banks, not including Commonwealth banks, in London in 1965, in comparison with 63 foreign banks in New York, 48 foreign banks in Paris and 17 foreign banks in Zurich.[15]

In 1976, despite the crisis in sterling and the financial markets, the United Kingdom applying for what was the then largest loan from the International Monetary Fund, the plan to eventually discontinue sterling as a reserve currency and the prohibition by the Bank of England on the use of sterling in the financing of trade not involving the United Kingdom, there was no effect on London as an international financial centre as it had by then been transformed into an offshore supranational financial centre where sterling had been replaced by eurocurrencies.[16]

These innovative markets have furthermore produced innovations in products and processes. Syndicated lending was introduced with one or more banks acting as lead manager and other banks as co-managers, underwriters or participants. Most of the business is conducted by banks in diverse locations through screen based trading. Syndicated lending is the largest proportion of eurocurrency lending, the other proportion being in the form of euronotes. Euro commercial paper, which is a short-term note and a means of cheaper funding than from a bank, and euro medium-term notes, underwritten by a bank and for a longer term than commercial paper, are termed euronotes. Certificates of deposit, an import from the United States, were introduced in the eurocurrency market in 1966. Euro certificates of deposit were developed by Citibank and were used for sourcing dollar funds with a negotiable instrument. This was an alternative to short-term deposits that were used to fund loans and that banks would roll-over to obtain the funds for longer terms.

Early innovations in systems included Euroclear, a clearing system that was established by Morgan Guaranty Trust Company in 1968 and a rival clearing system, Cedel, was established in 1970. The effect of this competition was to reduce fees. There were other significant innovations in the eurobond market in the 1970s, such as the floating rate note, first used in the issue of the Italian firm ENEL in 1970 and this may be considered as the first securitisation of assets.[17] Eurobanks act as intermediaries in the markets efficiently redistributing available funds between banks and non-bank surplus units and thereby performing an international liquidity function. They function due to lending rates being lower and deposit rates higher than the rates for the same currency in domestic markets.

The foreign exchange market

The euromarkets are closely linked to the foreign exchange market but the foreign exchange market is not part of the international money or capital markets. The Bretton Woods system consisted of the dollar as the pivotal currency with other currencies exchange rates fixed against the dollar with some small fluctuations permitted and allowances for revaluations or devaluations against the dollar. It is since the dollar was decoupled from gold that the foreign exchange market, as it is currently constituted, began to develop. The value and volume of transactions in the foreign exchange market has increased so much and are at such levels that central banks have insufficient reserves to intervene in the market as such an action would be futile in attempting to manage exchange rates.

Global foreign exchange market turnover, excluding that of derivatives markets, by type of transaction and type of dealer is outlined for the last 10 years in Table 2.1. The foreign exchange market, excluding derivatives markets, has increased by almost 68%, at constant exchange rates since 1995 despite a decline in trading in the 2001 survey.

A spot transaction is an exchange of two currencies for immediate delivery, that is, within two business days. An outright forward transaction is an exchange of two currencies at an agreed rate for delivery at a future date. A foreign exchange swap is an exchange of the principal amount only of two currencies for a specified period at an agreed exchange rate and a reverse exchange at maturity of the currencies at an exchange rate agreed when entering into the contract.

The principal dealers in the foreign exchange market are commercial banks, investment banks and securities firms that interact in the interdealer market and who also transact with governments, large firms and other financial institutions, trading for their own account and also providing foreign exchange services to customers. Investment funds,

Table 2.1 Global Foreign Exchange Market Turnover* 1995–2004 Daily Averages in April
US Dollar Billions and Percentage

Instrument	1995	1998	2001	2004	Percentage 2004
Spot Transactions	494	568	387	621	35
Outright Forwards	97	128	131	208	12
Foreign Exchange Swaps	546	734	656	944	53
Total turnover in year**	1,190	1,490	1,200	1,880	
Total at 2004 exchange rates	1,120	1,590	1,380	1,880	
Local percentage ***	46	46	43	38	
Cross-Border percentage ***	54	54	57	62	
With Reporting Dealers percentage ****	64	64	59	53	
With Other Financial Institutions percentage ****	20	20	28	33	
With non-Financial Customers percentage ****	16	17	13	14	

* Adjusted for local and cross-border double counting.
** The three instrument rows do not add to the total as they include estimated gaps in reporting. For 2004, the total before adding the estimated gap of $107 is $1,773.
*** Based on the total before adding estimated gaps. A cross-border transaction depends on the location and not the nationality of the counterparty.
**** The Bank for International Settlements separates large commercial and investment banks and securities firms, which are termed reporting dealers, from other commercial and investment banks and securities firms and investment funds, plan funds, mutual funds, insurance firms and corporate banks and financial subsidiaries of large firms, which are termed other financial institutions, and a third category of non-financial customers which includes those counterparties not included in the other categories, principally governments and firms.
Source: Bank for International Settlements, Triennial Central Bank Survey of Foreign Exchange and Derivatives Market Activity in April 2004, Preliminary Global Results, September 2004, Tables 1 and 2

mutual funds, plan funds, insurance firms and corporate banks and financial subsidiaries of large firms also participate.

Swaps by far comprise the largest amount of transactions at 53% of all transactions in 2004. In terms of counterparty for this type of instrument 60% were with reporting dealers and 73% were swaps for up to seven days, with 25% over seven days and up to a year. The dollar is by far the main currency traded accounting for 88.7% of the market with the euro accounting for 37.2%, the yen 20.3%, sterling 16.9% and the swiss franc 6.1%. This distribution is based on a total sum of 200% as there are counterparty currencies in transactions.[18]

The geographical distribution of foreign exchange trading is outlined in Table 2.2. The United Kingdom and the United States have more than 50% share of the total market turnover. These eight countries account for almost 80% of the total foreign exchange market turnover.

The leading banks in foreign exchange in the principal financial centres are outlined in Table 2.3. Citigroup, Deutsche Bank, United Bank of Switzerland, JPMorgan Chase, HSBC and Goldman Sachs are ranked in the three centres with Barclays Bank ranked in London and Tokyo and Morgan Stanley ranked in London and New York.

Table 2.2 Geographical Distribution of Foreign Exchange Market Turnover* 1998–2004
Selected Countries' Percentage Share

Leading Countries	1998 %	2001 %	2004 %
United Kingdom	32.5	31.2	31.3
United States	17.9	15.7	19.2
Japan	6.9	9.1	8.3
Singapore	7.1	6.2	5.2
Germany	4.8	5.5	4.9
Hong Kong	4.0	4.1	4.2
Australia	2.4	3.2	3.4
France	3.7	3.0	2.7
Total Selected Countries	79.3	78.0	79.2

* Adjusted for double-counting
Source: Bank for International Settlements, Triennial Central Bank Survey of Foreign Exchange and Derivatives Market Activity in April 2004, Preliminary Global Results, September 2004, Table 5

Table 2.3 Leading Banks in Foreign Exchange 2004

Rank	London	New York	Tokyo
1	Citigroup	Citigroup	Citigroup
2	Deutsche Bank	Deutsche Bank	JPMorgan Chase
3	UBS	UBS	Deutsche Bank
4	HSBC	JPMorgan Chase	Mitsubishi Tokyo
5	Barclays Bank	HSBC	UBS
6	Royal Bank of Scotland	Goldman Sachs	Goldman Sachs
7	Goldman Sachs	Bank of America	HSBC
8	JPMorgan Chase	Morgan Stanley	Barclays Bank
9	Dresdner	ABN-AMRO	Morgan Stanley
10	Morgan Stanley	Merrill Lynch	Mizuho Financial Group

Source: Euromoney, May 2004

The best foreign exchange banks, best foreign exchange research, and best online foreign exchange trading systems are also compiled by *Global Finance* based on surveys of analysts, management and technology experts. The criteria for selection include transaction share, global coverage, customer service, pricing and innovative technology. The leading banks are similar to the Euromoney ranking. The best foreign exchange bank in Europe is Deutsche Bank, while Citigroup was selected as the best foreign exchange bank in North America and Latin America. HSBC was considered the best foreign exchange bank in Asia Pacific and Standard Bank was considered the best in Africa. Bank of New York was considered to have the best foreign exchange research and United Bank of Switzerland the best bank system for online foreign exchange trading systems. In Europe, Deutsche Bank provides services in all areas of foreign exchange business. It is a leading participant globally with high volumes of business and is one of the leading three globally in terms of foreign exchange revenue. Citigroup deals in 150 currencies and has a worldwide presence. In the Americas it is represented in the United States, in all provinces in Canada, through its subsidiary, Banamex, in Mexico and in 21 countries in Latin America. HSBC has 20 dealing rooms in Asia and has 700 offices in 22 Asian countries. Like Citigroup it offers 24 hour global foreign exchange trading through its worldwide representation. Standard Bank is the largest South African bank and one of the leading banks in Africa where it is widely represented.[19]

Derivative financial products

Derivative financial products are based on future values of an asset and may be classified into three broad categories as forward and future based contracts, option based contracts and swaps. As the value of these contracts are based on the values of underlying assets, or an index of assets, such as bonds, equities, foreign currency or commodities, they are used for hedging, speculating, arbitrage and portfolio management. A derivative financial product is an agreement whereby payments are made between counterparties to the agreement depending on the fluctuations in the underlying asset prices. They have three broad characteristics; type of instrument, type of underlying asset and type of contract or trading method, that is, exchange traded or in an over-the-counter market.

The first exchange traded derivative financial product, foreign currency futures, was introduced by the Chicago Mercantile Exchange in 1972. By 1980 there were only five derivative financial product exchanges and four of these were in the United States. It was not until the 1980s that other exchanges opened in Europe and Asia. By 1990 American exchanges had 65% share of world volume in exchange traded derivatives with European exchanges having an 18% share, of which the London International Financial Futures Exchange, LIFFE, accounted for 8% alone, Japanese exchanges 13% and other Asian 4%.[20] The London International Financial Futures Exchange opened in 1982, the Marché à Terme International de France, MATIF, in 1986 and the Deutsche Terminbörse in 1990. The first Asian derivative exchange was the Singapore International Monetary Exchange. In Japan, derivatives trading developed when the Tokyo International Financial Futures Exchange was established in 1989.

Derivatives are off-balance sheet commitments for banks and the various types of contract, instrument and risk category are outlined in Figure 2.2. There are two types of contracts, three principal types of instruments and four main risk categories.

There are several fundamental differences between exchange traded contracts and over-the-counter contracts for derivatives. Exchange traded derivatives are standardised while the over-the-counter market is in customised derivative products. Exchanges are also organised and have standardised participating and trading rules with simultaneous buying and selling of contracts. The exchange manages counterparty risk and traders in effect trade with the exchange, a central counterparty, rather than bilaterally, and maintain margins with the exchange clearing system. Over-the-counter derivative products are customised and, therefore, have additional risk than exchange traded derivatives. As well as being a lower credit risk, exchange traded derivatives are also more liquid and have lower transaction costs due to standardisation.[21]

Trading Contract	Exchange	Over-the-Counter		
Instrument	Forward and Future	Option	Swap	
Risk Category	Interest Rate	Foreign Exchange	Equity Linked	Commodity

Figure 2.2 Derivative Contracts, Instruments and Risk Category Markets

A future is a standardised instrument to which parties agree to buy or sell a specified amount of a financial asset, such as currencies or equities, or a physical commodity, at a specified price at some agreed future date. As they are standardised instruments they may be traded. A currency future conveys the right to the exchange of a specific amount of currency for another currency at a specific date. A forward differs from a future in that it is not standardised and is an agreement to buy or sell at a specified future date an underlying financial asset at the spot price, that is, the price on the date of the contract.

An option allows a purchaser to exercise the right to buy, a call option, or the right to sell, a put option, a financial asset at the agreed price and at a specific date for European options, on or before a specific date for American options. There is no obligation to exercise the option. These instruments are also traded. A currency option gives the right to exchange an agreed amount of currency for another at a specified exchange rate and, similarly, an equity option conveys the right to buy or sell specific equities at an agreed price and date. An interest rate option is the right to pay or obtain an agreed interest rate over a specific period of time.

Another type of instrument, a swap, is an agreement to exchange payments of financial assets. A currency swap is an agreement between counterparties to exchange interest payments in different currencies for a specific period and to exchange the principal amount of the same currencies at maturity at a specified exchange rate. An interest rate swap transforms payments from different types of interest rate, such as a fixed interest rate into a floating rate, and is calculated on a notional principal amount which is not exchanged. A forward rate agreement allows one counterparty to obtain fixed interest rate payments while paying a floating interest rate and vice versa and is based on a notional principal amount for a specific period and commencing at an agreed future date.

Similar to the categorisation of dealers in the foreign exchange market, the Bank for International Settlements also differentiates between large commercial and investment banks and securities firms, which are termed reporting dealers, from a second category which includes other commercial and investment banks, other securities firms, investment funds, mutual funds, plan funds, insurance firms and corporate banks and financial subsidiaries of large firms, which collectively are termed other financial institutions, as well as from a third category consisting of non-financial customers which includes those counterparties not included in the other two categories, principally governments and other firms.

The main participants are banks as dealers and end-users, as well as other end-users, such as other financial firms including investment funds and hedge funds, and non-financial firms, such as, governments, supranational organisations and public authorities. End-users use derivative financial products for transferring risk and these include banks when proprietary trading. Banks are intermediaries in the over-the-counter market acting as a broker or counterparty as well as trading on their own account. They are exposed to risk as intermediaries and as end users. Exposure to risk and accurate valuations are difficult to assess as the underlying asset on which the derivative is based, whether directly or indirectly, fluctuates in value during the term of the derivative contract. Dealers are market makers who trade price information and risk is commoditised and traded. The leading derivative dealers in 2000 are outlined in Table 2.4.

Banks also establish highly capitalised and highly rated subsidiaries so as to gain a competitive advantage and obtain market share. The purpose of these derivative product companies is to separate the credit risk from the owning bank of derivative financial products and to guarantee transactions while the market risk is managed by the owning bank. As they are established for credit rating purposes they are essentially regulated by private credit rating agencies. They are highly credit rated and allow relatively lower

Table 2.4 Leading Derivative Dealers 2000

Bank	Rank
Citigroup	1
Goldman Sachs	2
Deutsche Bank	3
Morgan Stanley	4
United Bank of Switzerland*	5
Merrill Lynch	6
JPMorgan Chase**	7 and 8
Crédit Suisse	9
Bank of America	10

* Warburg
** JPMorgan ranked 7 and Chase ranked 8 in 2000 have since merged
Source: Schinasi, G., Craig, R., Drees, B., and Kramer, C., Modern Banking and OTC Derivatives Markets, International Monetary Fund, Washington, 2000, Table 2.1, p. 4

credit rated owning banks to transact business with end-users that require highly rated counterparties.

According to Siems comparative advantage is the basis for trade in derivative financial products as they allow the free trading of risk and it is information asymmetries that create the differences in the advantages.[22]

To measure the volume of derivates transaction a notional amount is used. This represents the size of the market and is not the exposure, the value of which is determined relative to market values and the cost of replacement. Market value represents the total value of contracts. Replacement value is the cost of replacing contracts at current prices. The notional and gross market values of over-the-counter derivatives markets by risk category are outlined in Table 2.5. The gross market value is a low percentage of the notional amount. Among the risk categories interest rate derivatives are the largest proportion.

The value of activity by instrument within the various risk categories is outlined in Table 2.6. Interest rate swaps dominate the interest rate risk category and forwards and forex swaps dominate the foreign exchange risk category, while options have the largest volume of activity in the equity linked and commodity risk categories.

The notional amount of the market in over-the-counter derivative foreign exchange contracts more than doubled since 2001. The currency share in 2004 in over-the-counter derivative markets turnover in foreign exchange currency swaps and options instruments is dominated by the dollar with 78.5% of the market and the Euro with 16% of the market.

Table 2.5 Global Over-the-Counter Derivatives Market 2003 Notional Amounts Outstanding and Gross Market Values by Risk Category US Dollar Billions and Percentage End Year

Risk category	Notional Amount	Gross Market Values	Gross Market Values as Percentage of Notional Amount	Leverage Ratio
Interest Rate	141,991	4,328	3.1	32.8
Foreign Exchange	24,484	1,301	5.3	18.8
Equity Linked	3,787	274	7.3	13.8
Commodity	1,406	128	9.1	11.0

Source: Bank for International Settlements, OTC Derivatives Market Activity in the Second Half of 2003, Monetary and Economics Department, 2004

Table 2.6 Global Over-the-Counter Derivatives Market 2003 Notional Amounts Outstanding by Risk Category and Instrument US Dollar Billions and Percentage End Year

Risk Category	Notional Amount	Instrument		
		Percentage	Percentage	Percentage
		Forward Rate Agreements	Interest Rate Swaps	Options
Interest Rate Contracts	141,991	7.6	78.3	14.1
		Forwards and Forex Swaps	Currency Swaps	Options
Foreign Exchange Contracts	24,484	50.6	26.0	23.4
			Forwards and Swaps	Options
Equity Linked Contracts	3,787		15.9	84.1
		Gold	Other Commodities	
			Forwards and Swaps	Options
Commodity Contracts	1,406	24.5	29.9	45.6

Source: Bank for International Settlements, Quarterly Review, June 2004, Table 19

The total notional amount of exchange-traded derivatives contracts at end 2003 was $36,734 billion, as outlined in Table 2.7, which is only a fifth of the over-the-counter market, although the markets are not perfectly comparable as there is a central counterparty in exchange-traded contracts. More than half of futures and of options are traded in North American exchanges. The majority of other futures and options are traded on European exchanges.

The emergence of derivative financial product markets has revolutionised the nature of financial intermediation with trading in interest rate, currency and equity products between banks and with other counterparties and have linked the global financial system through the linkages in underlying assets, interest rates and currencies leading to a more integrated system and also because the majority of trading is concentrated among the leading international banks and in a few international financial centres. The systemic consequences of having

Table 2.7 Global Exchange Traded Futures and Options Derivatives 2003 Amounts Outstanding by Risk Category, Notional Amount, Instrument and Location
US Dollar Billions and Percentage by Region End Year

Instrument	Notional Amount	Risk Category Interest Rate	Risk Category Currency	Risk Category Equity Linked
Futures	13,705	13,123	80	502
of which				
North America	56.2%			
Europe	31.8%			
Asia and Pacific	10.8%			
Other	1.2%			
Options	23,029	20,794	38	2,197
of which				
North America	51.3%			
Europe	48.0%			
Asia and Pacific	0.5%			
Other	0.2%			

Source: Bank for International Settlements, Quarterly Review, June 2004, Table 23 A

the leading banks as the main intermediaries must be considered as these same intermediaries are also the leading intermediaries in other financial markets and in several regions.

The gold market in London

Gold plays an important part throughout the development of international banking, especially in London. It was the basis for the gold standard, with the price of gold fixed against sterling, and the goldsmith was also the professional origin of one type of London banker. Mocatta and Goldsmid, now part of Scotiabank and one of the original five banks that have fixed the price of gold in London since 1919, was founded in 1684 and was by the late 18th century responsible for the Bank of England's gold operations. The current gold market has been located in London for most of the 20th century when in 1919 the main gold producing countries decided to sell gold through the market there. This continued until the outbreak of war in 1939. The price was fixed by representatives of five merchant banks, most notably N.M. Rothschild, which chaired the group, and Samuel Montagu.

The United States by refusing, in 1933, private transactions in gold and demanding the holders of gold to relinquish their stocks, a restriction in place for the following 42 years, allowed London to resume as the natural location for the market when it reopened in 1954. It resumed with the original five banks, continuing to be chaired by N.M. Rothschild as before, but with a different price of sterling to gold due to the devaluation of sterling in 1949. Following the reopening of gold fixing in London in 1954 a separate public gold market emerged in 1961 when central banks began to deal in gold on the London market, managed by the Bank of England. By then the price of gold was higher than the official price which had been since the Bretton Woods Agreement fixed at $35 an ounce and a gold pool was established by central banks to maintain this price by intervening in the market through the sale of central banks' gold holdings. This gold pool was increasingly under pressure from speculators who considered that it was becoming very difficult to maintain this price as the United States' balance of payments deficit worsened. Dollars flowed out of the United States' reserves in the attempt to hold the price. The practice was abandoned in 1968 and two markets emerged, the official market among central banks and the private market. In the meantime Zurich became a competitor market to London.

Investors and speculators were moving from the dollar to other currencies and there was so much pressure on the dollar speculation mounted that it would be devalued. The result was that the convertibility of dollars into gold was abandoned in 1971. The Smithsonian Agreement later that year devalued the dollar although the United States was not obliged to resume convertibility. Over the following two years pressure mounted on currencies and despite a further devaluation of the dollar, speculation continued until currencies began to freely float in 1973. In 1974, one of the banks that participated in the fixing of the gold price, the banking division of Johnson Matthey, was in difficulties after overextending its loan book. The Bank of England intervened in its restructuring, as well as persuading other banks to assist, partly to ensure that the gold market would not move to Zurich which was challenging London.

Rothschilds the chairing bank and the other banks, Kleinworths, which had acquired Sharps Pixley, Midland Bank, having acquired Samuel Montagu, Standard Chartered, having acquired Mocatta and Goldsmid, along with Johnson Matthey decided to re-constitute the system in 1987 and the London Bullion Association Market was established with a larger and more representative number of banks as members. The current market consists of bullion banks and the Bank of England operates the London Bullion Clearing. Trading in gold derivatives is conducted globally with most transaction in over-the-counter markets. The notional amount outstanding of derivative commodity contracts in the over-the-counter market in gold was $345 billion in 2003, almost a quarter of the total notional amount outstanding of all derivative commodity contracts.

All the original merchant banks, except Rothschilds which continued to chair the group until 2004 when it announced that it was withdrawing from gold trading, have been acquired by other banks and the current gold fixing group consists of Barclays having replaced Rothschilds as the chair bank, HSBC, having acquired Midland Bank, Scotiabank, Deutsche Bank, Republic Bank of New York, and Johnson Matthey.

Competition between intermediaries

The shift from loans into other forms of capital raising commenced in the 1970s. This was a period of high inflation. Due to interest rate limits investors shifted from deposits into mutual funds and there was a subsequent shortage of capital for lending by banks. Banks had an incentive to encourage their highly credit-rated customers to issue commercial paper and provided lines of credit as support. Commercial paper is a short-term unsecured promissory note and is an alternative form of raising short-term capital by large high quality credit rated firms to borrowing from banks.

There are three factors that impact on bank loans and open market paper according to Duca. These are bank regulatory taxes, implicit deposit insurance and the differential between the information cost of loans and of open market paper. The effect of an increase in banks' regulatory taxes increases the cost to banks of providing loans making them relatively more expensive. Reduced information costs of open market paper may be due to better information on issuers thereby reducing the cost of trading and the liquidity of commercial paper and bonds.[23] Between 1970 and 1991 commercial paper outstanding in the United States increased at an annual rate of 14%, with American non-bank financial firms being the largest issuer with 61.3% of the total outstanding in 1991. American non-financial firms' share was 18.7%, foreign financial firms' share was 10.5%, foreign non-financial firms' share was 4.9% and American banks' share was 4.6%.[24]

The development of money market mutual funds is closely linked to the increase of commercial paper outstanding. These open ended investment companies which in Europe are also termed unit trusts or collective investments in variable capital[25] were an alternative to bank deposits for investors and had been in existence since the 1930s. The amount of investment in such funds in the United States increased from less than $500 million in 1940 to $2.5 billion by 1950, though they only held 1% of securities listed on the New York Stock exchange. By the mid 1960s the number of funds was less than 200 whose assets were $35.2 billion although they increased slightly the proportion of their assets held as New York listed securities to less than 5%.[26] Correspondingly the share of equities outstanding held directly by individuals in the United States declined from 91% in 1952 to 53% in 1991.[27]

Money market mutual funds sought large denomination, short-term, high yield products in which to invest. Commercial paper was the perfect product such that by 1991 42% of the value of all money market mutual funds assets in the United States consisted of commercial paper issued in the United States and their holdings accounted for 36% of the value of all commercial paper outstanding there.[28] This was an American phenomenon. In the United States the total commercial paper issued in 1990 was $557.8 million, 63.5% of the total amount world commercial paper outstanding of $878.5 million.[29] Commercial paper outstanding at end 2003 was $418 billion, 26% of which was denominated in dollars, a decline in share from 32% in 2002, with 51% denominated in euro, an increase in share from 43%, and 15% in sterling, much the same share as in 2002.[30] Money market funds in the United States held $2.2 trillion in assets in 2002 of which $600 billion, 28%, consisted of commercial paper accounting for almost 44% of commercial paper issued by American firms.[31]

Sterling money market funds are much smaller in terms of amount invested than the equivalent dollar funds in the United States with assets in 2004 of approximately £42 billion. Money market funds in sterling are similar to the dollar funds in that a large proportion of their assets consist of commercial paper. The average portfolio composition in 2004 consists of 44% of funds held as commercial paper, which is a higher proportion than in dollar funds. The increase in the amount of commercial paper outstanding and the amount of assets in money market funds is highly positively correlated in the last five years. The investments in sterling money market funds are primarily by institutional investors. This is also a recent trend in the United States where the amount of wholesale funds' assets have increased at a faster rate than retail funds' assets whereby in 2003 the amount of wholesale funds' assets were slightly more than those of retail funds which have assets of almost $1 trillion.[32]

The interconnections in the financial markets between deficit and surplus units, indirectly through intermediaries and funds, and also directly, are illustrated in Figure 2.3. This excludes governments, public authorities and supranational agencies which are funded primarily through the wholesale money market and through issuing bonds in the capital markets. There are two types of firms. Issuing firms are those that issue equities, commercial paper and bonds and other firms are firms that issue equities only. Financial firms also issue paper and, of course, commercial and investment banks also manage their own funds but these are not included.

Firms and individuals deposit surplus funds which commercial banks use to make loans. These units also borrow from commercial banks. Firms issue equities and those firms with high credit quality also issue short-term commercial paper and medium and long-term bonds. They are purchased directly by money market mutual funds, institutional investors, asset managers and other firms and individuals. Individuals also purchase shares

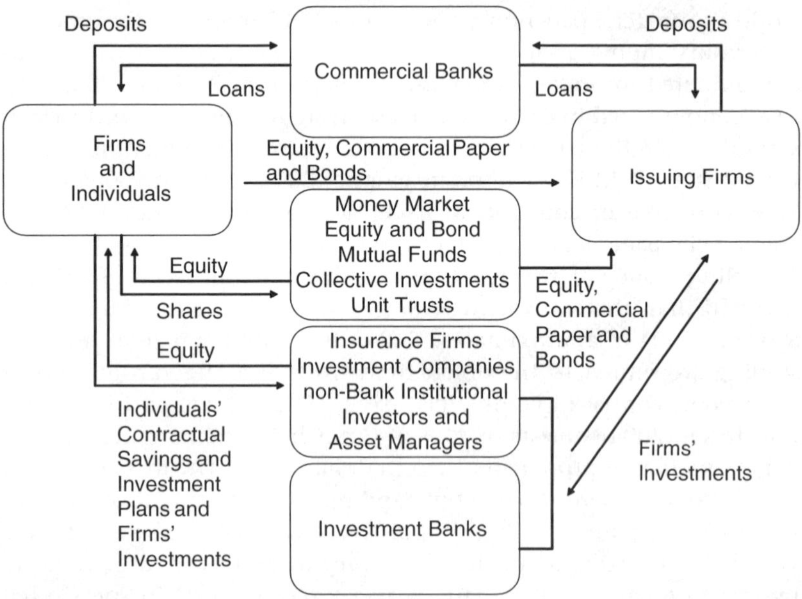

Figure 2.3 Alternative Sources of Funding among Private Sector Units
Source: based on Duca, How Low Interest Rates Impact Financial Institutions, Federal Reserve Bank of Dallas, Southwest Economy, Issue 6, 2003, p. 9

in money market mutual funds and in bond mutual funds and these funds purchase equities, commercial paper and bonds issued by large high credit quality firms. In addition, individuals may also have contractual savings and investment plans. Similarly, firms may have various investments with institutional investors which also invest in equities, commercial paper and bonds. Of course, surplus units may also purchase equities in firms and commercial paper and bonds from issuing firms without using mutual funds or other intermediaries. Investment banks underwrite and distribute issues and are also actively involved in trading issues in secondary markets. Banks are in competition for firms and individuals' surplus funds, as well as with investment companies, open and closed ended investment companies, insurance firms and investment plan funds.

The influence of institutional investors

Institutional investors play an increasingly significant role in international financial markets as competitors to banks in sourcing funds. They are influential in terms of the amount of funds they have available for investment and that they are often the major shareholders in banks and other firms. The main types of institutional investors are insurance firms, plan funds and investment companies. Tables 2.8 and 2.9 outline the variations in the financial assets of institutional investors in selected countries and by type of institutional investor respectively.

Table 2.8 Financial Assets of Institutional Investors 2001
US Dollar Billions and Percentage of Gross Domestic Product Selected Countries*

Country	Amount	Percentage
Belgium	244.3	109.0
France	1,701.3	131.8
Germany	1,478.4	81.0
Italy	1,007.6	94.0
Netherlands	722.2	190.9
Spain	355.2	61.9
United Kingdom	2,743.3	190.9
Switzerland	575.5	232.7
United States	19,257.7	191.0
Canada	794.3	115.8
Japan	3,644.8	94.7

* These countries account for 92.5% of the total financial assets of institutional investors in 28 member countries of the Organisation for Economic Cooperation and Development, OECD.
Source: Organisation for Economic Cooperation and Development, Institutional Investors Yearbook, 2003, Tables S.1 and S.6.

Table 2.9 Financial Assets of Institutional Investors by Type of Institutional Investor 2001
US Dollar Billions and Percentage of Total

Institutional Investor	Amount	Percentage
Insurance Firms	11,342	25.9
Plan Funds	9,564	29.4
Investment Companies	11,280	34.9
Other	2,972	9.8
Total 28 OECD Countries	35,158	100

Source: Organisation for Economic Cooperation and Development, Institutional Investors Yearbook, 2003, Tables S.1, S.2, S.3, S.4 and S.5

Investment companies have the largest proportion of assets with over a third of the total although the proportions between the different types of institutional investor do not differ significantly.

The majority of institutional investors in the countries selected hold a large proportion of their portfolio as bonds with some notable exceptions, such as, the Netherlands, Switzerland, the United Kingdom and the United States, as outlined in Table 2.10. Loans are a large proportion of the portfolio of institutional investors in Germany and Japan.

The average annual growth rates between 1993 and 2001 of financial assets of all institutional investors in 28 OECD countries, as outlined in Table 2.11, was 9%, with investment companies increasing by 15%, plan funds by 8% and insurance companies by 7%. In 1993 investment

Table 2.10 Portfolio Composition of Institutional Investors 2001
Percentage

Country	Bonds	Shares	Loans	Other
Belgium	40.0	41.0	5.0	14.0
France	47.0	43.0	3.0	7.0
Germany	42.0	24.0	28.0	6.0
Italy	54.0	18.0	0.0	27.0
Netherlands	31.0	43.0	15.0	11.0
Spain	49.0	24.0	2.0	22.0
United Kingdom	15.0	65.0	1.0	19.0
Switzerland	37.0	41.0	14.0	8.0
United States	35.5	44.0	9.0	11.0
Canada	39.0	25.0	5.0	30.0*
Japan	56.0	16.0	21.0	7.0

* Including 19% in foreign securities
Not all add to 100%
Source: Organisation for Economic Cooperation and Development, Institutional Investors Yearbook, 2003, Table S.11

companies held 23% of total financial assets and this increased to 32% in 2001 with a corresponding decline from 38% held by insurance firms to 32% in the same period. Plan funds share of total financial assets increased 2% and other types of institutional investors declined by 1%. During this period shares increased by 11.6% as a proportion of financial assets held by all institutional investors, bonds increased by 6.9%, loans by 1.7% and other types of financial assets by 8.9%.

Individuals' claims on institutional investors as a proportion of their total financial assets are outlined in Table 2.12. Individuals in the United Kingdom, the United States and Belgium have the largest proportions, with those in Japan the lowest proportion. These are significant proportions, neverthcless, in the selected countries and illustrate the importance of institutional investors in the competition between financial firms for individuals' investments.

Table 2.11 Total Financial Assets by Type of Institutional Investor 1993–2001 Percentage of Total and Average Annual Growth Rate

Institutional Investor	Percentage	Percentage	Average Annual Growth Rate 1993–2001 Percentage
Insurance Firms	38	32	7
Investment Companies	23	32	15
Plan Funds	29	27	8
Other	10	9	7
Total Institutional Investors	100	100	9

Source: Organisation for Economic Cooperation and Development, Institutional Investors Yearbook, 2003, Chart 1, p. 15, Chart 2, p. 15, Chart 6, p. 31

Table 2.12 Individuals' Claims on Institutional Investors 2001 Percentage of Total Outstanding Financial Assets of Individuals

Country	Percentage
Belgium	26.2
France	26.7
Germany	35.7
Italy	21.4
Netherlands	53.9
United Kingdom**	52.0
United States	39.3
Canada	33.0
Japan	27.5

** 1995

Source: Organisation for Economic Cooperation and Development, Institutional Investors Yearbook, 2001 and 2003, Table S.12

Capital flows

While innovations in products have linked international financial markets, liberalisation of financial markets and the abolishment of exchange controls have been catalysts for the increase in capital flows. These flows are financing current account deficits, in particular in recent years in industrialised countries, especially the United States. Capital flows also consist of foreign direct investment and this comprises much of the flows in recent years. The current account balances for developed countries and the total world are outlined in Table 2.13.

The gross value of foreign capital stock in developing countries, in 1990 prices, was $235.4 billion in 1914 and this declined to $63.2 billion by 1950. There was rapid growth in developing economies from the mid 1950s and 1960s, coinciding with many of these countries' recently obtained independence, and official development assistance was unable to meet the demand for capital. Real national product of developing economies increased 5.5% annually in aggregate in the 1960s, increasing to almost 6% annually in the 1970s. By 1973 foreign capital stock in developing countries had increased to $495.2 billion and by 1998 to $3,030.7 billion in 1990 prices.[33]

There was a noticeable decline in the share of official development assistance as a proportion of the financial flows to developing countries in the 1970s, a trend which had already commenced in the 1950s, as outlined in Table 2.14. This trend continued in the early 1980s with a large increase in financial flows. The amount in 1981 alone was double the total for the 1970s. However, the total amount in individual years between 1981 and 1985 declined by almost 40% and official development assistance remained the same, such that it had a higher proportion of the total, being 27.4% in 1981 and increasing to 44% in 1985, although for this period the proportion is lower than in previous periods.

Table 2.13 Current Account Balances 1991–2004
US Dollar Billions

Region	Average 1991–2000	2001	2002	2003	2004*
European Union	9	–6	67	36	48
United States	–150	–394	–481	–542	–496
Japan	107	88	113	138	144
World	–80	–169	–110	–121	–99

* International Monetary Fund forecast
Source: Bank for International Settlements, Annual Report, 2004, Table II.7, p. 29

Table 2.14 Financial Flows to Developing Countries 1956–1985 US Dollar Billions in 1980 Dollars*

	Total	of which Official Development Assistance	Official Development Assistance as a Percentage of Total
1956–1960	21.9	13.2	60.3
1961–1970	29.0	16.2	55.9
1971–1980	76.6	28.1	36.7
1981–1985	542.7	182.8	33.7

* Data between periods are not perfectly comparable due to re-definition. The dollar is deflated by the gross national product deflator for industrial countries with exchange rates constant from 1981.
Source. Fishlow, A., in Van Der Wee, H. and Aerts, E. (eds), Debates and Controversies in Economic History, Presses Universitaire de Louvain, 1990, Table 4, p. 156

Banks had been attracted to sovereign lending to developing countries due to the availability of funds, especially petro-dollars, and the higher returns that were available. There were no international defaults since the 1930s and the immediate post-war period and banks were pursuing a herd mentality approach in their sovereign lending. Syndicates were formed and many smaller follower banks entered this market and depended on the lead banks to assess the risk for them, and which they considered would be lower due to syndication. Competition, however, reduced margins and banks were lending long term at low interest rates. Many of the loans were repeat loans which reduced the marginal cost of these through previous assessment and monitoring and also reduced the risk of default.

Following the announcement by Mexico, despite being an oil producer and the beneficiary of high oil prices in the 1970s, and other countries, most notably Poland, that they were unable to continue servicing loans there was a crisis in sovereign lending, to what at the time were termed less developed countries, which banks, heretofore, had considered as relatively low risk lending. The developing countries were also affected by the large oil price increases in the 1970s and by the monetary policies of most of the industrialised countries, especially the interest rate management policies. The relatively higher interest rates increased their repayments. The International Monetary Fund intervened in the crisis assisting in the rescheduling of loans and, with the cooperation of banks by refinancing, although its conditional concomitant stabilising economic reforms increased pressure on these developing countries and other initiatives, such as debt for equity swaps agreements and bond agreements, proposed in two separate periods in the mid to late 1980s by different American Secretaries of State assisted in resolving the crisis by encouraging and promoting plans for the restructuring and reduction of loans.

Banks reassessed their exposures to developing economies. The most notable differences in the type of capital flows to developing countries in the 1980s has been the decline in the share of commercial bank loans, which was 46% of the total in 1981 and 13.6% in 1992. Portfolio equities investments increased from 0.1% to 5.7% and bonds increased from 1.2% to 9.4% with foreign direct investment doubling from 8.3% to 16.7% in the same period. Official development assistance was the same proportion at 26%.[34]

There was a renewed interest in emerging economies in the 1990s and net private capital flows peaked at an average of $94 billion a year in 1995–1996 compared to $44 billion in 2002. This may be partly explained by the establishment and development of foreign offices by European and American banks in some emerging markets, especially in Latin America and in central and eastern Europe, whereby local claims on emerging markets increased from 14% of foreign banks' claims in 1995 to 40% in 2002, a tenfold increase in constant 2002 dollar terms, and amounting to $544 billion in 2002.[35]

The data for net capital flows to developing and transition economies, since 2000, is outlined in Table 2.15. It is clear that private

Table 2.15 Net Private and Official Capital Flows to Developing and Transition Economies 2000–2003
US Dollar Billions

Developing Economies	**2000**	**2001**	**2002**	**2003**
Total Private Capital Flows	23.9	27.3	12.9	82.9
of which				
Private Direct Investment	149.7	161.4	112.0	102.5
Private Portfolio Investment	8.5	–86.3	–91.1	–78.1
Other Private Capital Flows*	–134.4	–47.9	–8.0	58.3
Official Flows	–13.8	23.0	11.6	2.7
Transition Economies	**2000**	**2001**	**2002**	**2003**
Total Private Capital Flows	18.3	–6.7	34.1	48.3
of which				
Private Direct Investment	25.3	27.7	27.3	16.8
Private Portfolio Investment	–2.4	–9.4	–7.5	–9.4
Other Private Capital Flows*	–4.6	–24.9	14.3	41.0
Official Flows	–0.7	2.8	–8.3	–9.9

* includes companies' long-term and short-term net investments

Source: United Nations Conference on Trade and Development, Trade and Development Report, 2004

direct investment is the largest proportion of these private flows to developing economies. However, certain developing regions attract much higher private capital flows than others, especially east and south east Asia, and in particular China and India, where private capital flows to both these countries amounted to $101.8 billion in 2003, an increase from $44.7 billion in 2002, and $43.0 billion in 2001. However, there were large increases in the net accumulation of foreign currency, $320.9 billion for developing economies, of which China purchased $117.1 billion and India purchased $31.7 billion of foreign currency. This offset net private capital flows. The outcome was total net outflows of $200 billion for developing economies.[36]

The proportion of total inward and outward stocks of foreign direct investment in services by the financial sector was 29% and 34% respectively in 2002. However, for the financial sector 77% of this inward foreign direct investment and 93% of the outward foreign direct investment were by firms from developed economies. The United States' imports of financial services were valued at $9 billion and its exports at $20 billion in 2002, of which intra-firm trade accounted for 60% of imports and 20% of exports of financial services.[37]

In 2001, banks' assets in foreign affiliates in developing economies as a proportion of total bank assets in these countries were, among Latin America countries, 82.7% in Mexico, 31.8% in Argentina, 29.8% in Brazil, and were, among central and eastern European countries, 90% in the Czech Republic, 88.8% in Hungary and 68.7% in Poland. Among developing economies in Africa and Asia the proportions were 53.5% in Ghana, 39.3% in Kenya, 7.7% in South Africa and 2.0% in China. The ratio is much lower in developed economies with the exception of the United Kingdom and the United States. The data for banks' assets in selected countries is outlined in Table 2.16.

The level of ownership of banks by foreign banks in selected emerging economies is outlined in Table 2.17. The Czech Republic and Mexico have the highest percentage of foreign ownership. This is mostly due to European banks acquiring Czech banks, such as the acquisistion of Komercni Banka by Société Générale, and to an American bank, Citigroup, acquiring Banamex and a European bank, BBVA acquiring Bancomer in Mexico where both these banks dominate the Mexican banking market.

The ten leading emerging market destinations in terms of share of total emerging market foreign direct investment by German banks' in

Table 2.16 Percentage of Foreign Bank Affiliates'* Assets to Total Assets 2001 Selected Countries

	Percentage
Developed Countries	
United Kingdom	46.0
United States	20.2
Switzerland	10.7
Spain	8.5
Japan**	6.7
Italy	5.7
Canada	4.8
Germany	4.3
Netherlands	2.2
Central and Eastern Europe	
Czech Republic	90.0
Hungary	88.8
Poland	68.7
Developing Economies Offshore Centres	
Singapore	76.0
Bahrain	72.0
Hong Kong	72.0
Developing Economies	
Mexico	82.7
Ghana	53.5
Kenya	39.3
Argentina	31.8
Brazil	29.8
South Africa	7.7
China	2.0

* Affiliates with more than 50% ownership including branches and representative offices
** 2002 Commercial banks only
Source: United Nations Conference on Trade and Development, World Investment Report, New York and Geneva, 2004, Table A.III.4

2001 are Poland 20%, Hong Kong 19%, Singapore 17%, Brazil 11%, Korea 10%, Hungary 7%, the Czech Republic 6%, Russia 4% and Mexico and India 3% each. In 1994 Poland was not among the leading destinations, though Argentina was ranked fourth and banks seem to have interrupted their direct investments there before the recent financial system crisis and switched to other destinations. Singapore and Hong Kong were the most favoured with 30% and 23% share of German banks' total emerging market foreign direct investment, respectively, in 1994 and have maintained their status as

Table 2.17 Foreign Bank Ownership* in Emerging Economies 2001 Central and Eastern Europe and Latin America Selected Countries

Country	Percentage
Central and Eastern Europe	
Czech Republic	93.0
Hungary	68.8
Poland	63.6
Latin America	
Mexico	76.5
Argentina	54.5
Brazil	30.6

**Note*: Foreign bank ownership refers to the ownership of more than 50% of total equity
Source: Wezel, T., Foreign Bank Entry into Emerging Economies: An Empirical Assessment of the Determinants and Risks Predicated on German FDI Data, Discussion Paper 1/2004, Series 1, Studies of the Economic Research Centre, Deutsche Bundesbank, 2004, Table 6, p. 28

among the most favoured destinations. Foreign direct investment by German non-banks firms has a strong influence on the foreign location decisions of German banks in emerging economies, along with the level of development of the country's financial market and the country's risk rating.[38]

3
Regulation, Trade Agreements, Consolidation and Integration in International Banking

While a significant proportion of deregulation of banking markets was implemented in the 1980s there was a closely associated re-regulation in the form of international banking industry accords. The European Union member states' financial markets were principally reformed by legislation, that is, through directives and recommendations. A single European financial market is due to be in place in 2005. The principle of home country control was introduced along with the equalisation of banking activities by specifying the permitted banking activities. By allowing banks from other member states to provide commercial and investment banking services in other member states, universal banking was effectively introduced as the standard type of banking, as member states were obliged to allow their indigenous banks to provide the same range of services or they would have been at a competitive disadvantage. The North American free trade agreement, NAFTA, was signed by the United States, Canada and Mexico. A separate Annex on Financial Services was agreed as part of the Uruguay round of the General Agreement on Tariffs and Trade, GATT, in the General Agreement on Trade in Services, GATS. Along with liberalisation in trade in banking services reducing the level of barriers to market access by foreign banks and the reform of banking systems through deregulation and re-regulation there has been the accompanied process of securitisation, which has progressed the process of globalisation and integration in banking. The recent increase in mergers between and acquisition of banks within and between countries has been mostly due to the single financial market and economic and monetary union in Europe, de-regulation in the United States and de-regulation, as well as, restructuring in Japan.

The external factors that influence a bank's policies and strategies may be categorised as regulatory and insurance conditions, market conditions, such as competitiveness and the diversity of products and services, and macroeconomic policies.[1]

Deregulation of financial markets

The relaxation of exchange controls in 1979 which had been in place in the United Kingdom since 1939 opened London for foreign lending in sterling and attracted investors into sterling as a means of diversification. This was soon followed by reform of the Stock Exchange regulations and member firms' activities. The reform was prompted by competition motives and also due to the increased volumes of business. This was one of the largest reforms of any sector, in this instance the British securities business and the Stock Exchange, in any of the international financial centres and was concluded in 1986. These reforms went further than those in New York in the 1970s and included amendments to the commission rates, the activities of the firms' business in share dealing and, significantly, they allowed banks acquire these firms leading to a new landscape in the City of London. The outcome was the sale of most of the leading British member firms of the Stock Exchange. In addition many of the merchant banks were competing directly with much larger American investment banks and now continental European universal banks and also with British commercial banks that entered this business through their own investment banking subsidiaries. Eventually most of these independent merchant banks would be purchased by continental European and American banks.

France, having nationalised the main banks and the Banque de France in 1945, introduced a policy of nationalisation of the other banks in the early 1980s which was against the trend in most developed countries. This policy was reversed quite soon afterwards commencing in 1987 with the privatisation of some banks. Another important reform of the banking system, which had commenced in the late 1960s by eliminating some of the distinctions between commercial and investment banks, was the Banking Act in 1984, eventually according the same status to commercial banks and investment banks.[2]

Domestically, although it affected foreign banks in the United States also, the State of Maine allowed inter-state acquisition on a national reciprocal basis in 1978. This was the first state to relax the restrictions imposed by the McFadden Act introduced in 1927 to ensure equal treatment of national and state chartered banks in branching and which limited interstate banking. During the following 20 years there was constant debate and proposals for deregulation and reform of financial markets which had been separated geographically by state. Although interstate banking was allowed on a reciprocal basis between states, eventually the Riegle-Neal Interstate Banking and Branching Efficiency Act in 1994 repealed the McFadden Act, though there are restrictions on banks' market shares within states and nationally.

The International Banking Act was enacted in the United States in 1978 as a response to certain competitive advantages that foreign banks had over domestic banks in the United States. The main effects were that foreign banks were required to nominate a state as its home state and that expansion into other states had to be by acquisition. There was also a reciprocity clause that allowed foreign banks entry in to the United States where American banks were allowed entry into the foreign bank's country. International Banking Facilities were introduced in 1981 to allow banks to conduct banking without being subject to interest rate restrictions and were intended for banks operating in offshore business such as the euromarkets, essentially an attempt to establish offshore business in New York. These entities, similar to those in the Japan Offshore Market, are considered resident in the country of location. In 1991 the Foreign Bank Enforcement Supervision Act was introduced ensuring foreign banks are regulated in the same manner as domestic banks. An important Securities and Exchange Commission amendment, Rule 144A, was introduced in 1990 relaxing certain registration requirements to encourage investment by institutional investors in American firms' securities. Throughout the 1980s and 1990s there had been some relaxation by regulators of the interpretation of the regulations on banks culminating in the Financial Services Modernisation Act in 1999, also known as the Gramm-Leach-Bliley Act, creating what is termed a Financial Holding Company. This repealed the Glass-Steagall Act which had delineated the banking industry between commercial and investment banking.

With the relaxation in 1972 of the Japanese regulation prohibiting its banks lending to foreigners, Japanese banks soon established offices in London to participate in syndicated lending. They came with large reserves of dollars obtained from Japanese multinational firms, among the largest in the world, and soon the price of borrowing was reduced as the Japanese banks arranged loans at lower interest rates.[3] The main divisions in the banking system within Japan have been based on products and customers. This was characterised by the separation of banks and securities firms, and among banks characterised by the separation between long-term and short-term banks and between customer types, such as, large non-financial firms and small and medium sized non-financial firms.

Banks are allowed to conduct business in what is termed the Japanese Offshore Market. Since 1973 Japanese commercial banks have been allowed to establish securities firms through foreign subsidiaries.

Liberalisation of the Japanese financial markets commenced in the early 1970s with the issue of yen and foreign currency denominated bonds by non-residents and also by allowing some foreign securities firms to become members of the Tokyo Stock Exchange. There has been significant restructuring in the banking industry and the largest mergers have been between Bank of Tokyo and Mitsubishi Bank in 1996 and between Dai-Ichi Kangyo, Fuji Bank and the Industrial Bank of Japan to form Mizuho Bank in 2000. The reforms in Japan though have not been as radical as the reforms in the United Kingdom and in the United States, with the Japanese government continuing to subsidise banks' recapitalisation, although there are some further reforms to be implemented which would reduce the interventionist role of government in banking and these include a planned limit on deposit insurance and the abolition of the Industrial Revitalisation Corporation which would reduce support of Japanese banks with public funds.

Capital adequacy

One of the purposes of bank capital adequacy regulations is to internalise systemic costs, such as, the cost to government of supporting banks through deposit insurance and costs to other banks when there is a bank default. This regulation should be accompanied by developing policies that promote and support banks to become more efficient in their lending.[4]

Banks are regulated for capital adequacy by their respective regulatory authorities although different methods have been used in different countries. With deregulation of banking eliminating some of the restrictions on banking activities by different types of banks within countries and the liberalisation and subsequent internationalisation of banking through reduced barriers to foreign market access there was a requirement to harmonise capital adequacy regulations between countries and to agree a common standard, not least to eliminate competitive advantages that banks from some countries may have had due to these differences. Capital adequacy regulations have been harmonised internationally since the late 1980s when the Basel Committee on Banking Supervision, established by the Bank for International Settlements, published what was known as the Basel Accord on capital adequacy. This was an initial attempt to implement uniform capital standards. The main provisions of the accord defined bank capital as Tier 1, bank equity, and, Tier 2, other additional sources of capital, and agreed risk weightings for specific asset categories and off-balance sheet items. The provisions also set a minimum risk based capital assets ratio with which banks were obliged to comply. These capital adequacy regulations have been implemented in almost all countries and are effectively a global standard.

There were limitations to the accord as it did not differentiate between the qualities of assets in any specific category and did not include other types of risks to which banks are subject. It also had the effect of banks manipulating their activities to conform to the standard while increasing business by focusing on aspects that had a lower risk weighting. Banks reduced their balance sheet assets in order to comply with capital adequacy requirements, to release capital for other purposes or to reduce their exposure to certain sectors or types of assets.

When certain types of loans were considered to be a lower risk than that implied by capital adequacy regulations then banks had an incentive to securitise them. Securitisation is the sale of financial assets based on future cash flows as tradable securities and sold in capital markets and the transfer of risk to the performance of the assets that have been securitised.[5] The quality of the remaining balance sheet assets could be affected depending on the type and quality of the assets in the bank's portfolio of assets that were securitised. There is also an unbundling of a bank's functions when securitising assets. For instance, by originating assets, assessing the risk and selling those assets on, banks are realising a competitive advantage in marketing, risk assessment and monitoring. The intermediation role of banks has been transformed through securitisation and banks may specialise in certain functions in which they consider they have a competitive advantage.

A subsequent accord, referred to as Basel II, was agreed in 2004 and based on three factors, namely, capital requirements, supervisory review and market discipline. Minimum capital requirements focus on credit, operational and trading risk. The principles of the accord are that national regulators shall continue to have a legal responsibility to regulate their domestic banks, although recognising that closer cooperation and coordination between the respective regulators is required. Home country regulators are responsible for implementing the accord on a consolidated basis while recognising the role of host country regulations, specifically when banks operate as subsidiaries. It also incorporates the principle that home country regulators should cooperate with other countries' regulators and avoid unnecessary regulation, and that regulators' roles be clearly defined.[6]

The concept of an internal rating based approach of the Basel II accord is a significant advancement on Basel I and is intended to reduce the amount of capital that a bank must hold for specific risk categories. In a survey in 2003 of foreign bank branches in London more than 70% stated that they would implement their own advanced internal ratings while most of the others stated that they would implement the standard internal ratings based approach which is through external credit rating agencies. In addition, 60% of respondents stated that an effect of the introduction of Basel II would be the holding of the same or more capital, with 28% responding that the effect would be the holding of less capital.[7] One of the arguments against the accord is that when a bank's capital base is affected by economic conditions, and subsequent lending quality, the bank's total loan portfolio is also regraded thereby requiring it to hold more capital.[8]

Liberalisation, international trade agreements and international banking

Liberalisation in the banking industry has been a feature of international banking since the 1980s. The European Union proposals for a single European market were published in 1985 in a White Paper, entitled 'Completing the Internal Market', and the Single European Act was enacted in 1986, eliminating barriers to trade and establishing free movement of goods, services, capital and labour within the European Union, with effect from 1992. This Act was followed by the Maastricht Treaty in 1992 which established a single market in the European Union, as well as, leading to Economic and Monetary Union in 1999 and a single currency, the euro, introduced in 2002, though exchange rates had been fixed in 1999 for participating member states' currencies. Prior to that two directives aimed specifically at the banking sector were the First Banking Co-ordination Directive in 1977, focusing on establishment of banks in other member states and based on the principle of host country control, and the Second Banking Co-ordination Directive in 1989, focusing on the harmonisation of prudential regulation of banks, mutual recognition by regulators of the application of the regulations on banks based on the principle of home country control, and the specification of the activities in which banks could provide services.

The specified services that banks may provide are essentially the main services provided by commercial and investment banks. Some member states allowed their banks to provide a wider range of services, that is, universal banking, than other member states allowed their banks to provide and therefore there was a competitive advantage for these universal type banks when transacting business in some member states. The Second Banking Co-ordination Directive thus permitted universal banking, that is, the possibility to provide both commercial and investment banking services by the same bank and this became the standard model of banking within the European Union, thereby ensuring that there would be deregulation and equalisation in the range of services that all banks in all member states could provide and effectively forcing member states, where commercial and investment banks were separate entities by practice, regulation or law, to deregulate their banking markets so as to minimise the disadvantages for their banks *vis-à-vis* some other member states' banks that could provide a broader range of services.

In terms of cross-border trade in financial services the effect of these initiatives was an increase in trade especially in off-balance sheet activities, investment management and in corporate lending. There was an increase of 58% in the establishment of cross-border branches between 1992 and 1995 and 11 member states notified the Commission of an intent to establish or acquire credit institutions in other member states during the same period. The cost of supplying cross-border services has also declined.[9]

The North American Free Trade Agreement came into effect in 1994 and liberalised restrictions on cross-border trade and foreign direct investment between these countries including the liberalisation of restrictions on the provision of banking services. This agreement superseded previous bilateral agreements between these countries and it is the 1989 bilateral Free Trade Agreement between the United States and Canada that is the basis for it, though widening its scope and extending it to Mexico. While it does not extend as far as the provisions of the Maastricht Treaty it has the objective of a single unified market in terms of market access.

The Uruguay round of the General Agreement on Tariffs and Trade commenced in 1986 and for the first time, following initiatives by the United States and the United Kingdom, included trade in services, including financial services, with the General Agreement on Trade in Services, GATS, completed in 1995.

These agreements reflect the trend to more liberalised trade and deregulation in national markets as well as a convergence towards global harmonisation of regulation, such as the capital adequacy regulations issued by the Bank for International Settlements. Thus liberalisation was linked to reform.

The approach to national treatment in trade agreements may be either *de facto* or *de jure*. *De facto* legislation allows for potential inequalities in competition between domestic and foreign firms when applying regulations. *De jure* national treatment applies regulations equally to domestic and foreign firms, whereas *de facto* treatment could be contravened although complying with *de jure* national treatment, as foreign firms could be at a competitive disadvantage to domestic firms due to, for example, market dominance and a bias towards domestic firms.[10]

The European Union approach of home country control contrasts with that of the NAFTA approach of host country control. The GATS follows a service, or product, approach, as does the European Union's Second Banking Co-Ordination Directive, outlining a broad range of banking services permissible, whereas the financial services chapter of NAFTA regulations focus more on institutions. This has been one of the reasons for the blurring of activities between commercial and investment banks and for the emergence of universal banking as the standard model. A service approach outlines the services that may be provided and between different types of banks and non-bank banks while the institutional approach focuses on those institutions providing the service.

The euro is an additional factor in the closer integration of financial markets in the European Union since official fixed exchange rates were agreed in 1999 and an integral part of economic and political union, though not all member states are in the Euro zone. Despite initiatives, in the almost 20 years since the single market proposals, retail commercial banking markets continue to be segmented on a geographic basis by member state. There has been more progress in wholesale banking markets integration.

A Financial Services Action Plan was implemented to introduce directives and regulations to overcome the barriers to integration in both retail and wholesale financial markets. The European Union is planning for the integration of financial services and the creation of a single financial market in 2005. The Financial Services Action Plan has three main objectives. These are to implement a single wholesale financial services market for corporate issuers, securities trading business and investment fund services and an integrated retail financial services market based on consumer protection and reduced barriers to the provision of financial services including a retail cross border payments system. The third objective relates to prudential rules and supervision for wholesale and retail banking services. Legislation is by means of directives and regulations. Some of the most important directives for the banking industry are the Undertaking for Collective Investment in Transferable Securities (UCITS) Directive in 2002, replacing that of 1985 and focusing on the type of assets in which mutual funds may invest, an amended Investment Services Directive to replace the 1993 directive, the Distance Marketing Directive on the sale of retail financial services in 2002, the Financial Conglomerates Directive of 2002 relating to the supervision of conglomerates and the Electric Commerce Directive in 2000 which provides a legal context for e-financial services. In addition, there are separate committees for regulations relating to banking, insurance and securities and on financial conglomerates.

The European Union is following a mandatory regulatory approach, as opposed to a system of regulatory competition, although there is some regulatory competition effect in practice due to the home country control principle whereby a firm recognised in one member state may provide the same services with no restrictions in other member states.[11] All barriers, however, cannot be removed by legislation. Some are dependent on the organisational structure of member states' banking markets and the conduct of these markets and that of the banks operating in these markets.

The outcome of harmonisation, mutual recognition and home country control along with open access to other member states' financial markets has been mixed. While they have created the possibility of a single financial market in the European Union, a possible contestable market, there are other barriers that must be overcome and that can not be legislated for. These include preferences among customers, national loyalty, bank loyalty and switching costs from one bank to another on the part of customers, along with asymmetric information and knowledge on the part of banks and local banking customs.

The purpose of NAFTA as it relates to financial services is to eliminate barriers to trade and allow banks and other financial service providers access to other signatory countries' markets. Specifically it allows banks and other financial firms to acquire or establish wholly-owned banks and securities firms in each other's countries. Subsidiaries of foreign banks are treated on a *de facto* basis. The agreement also allows for cross-border provision of financial services without establishing in the country of the customer, although in this instance it cannot solicit business. It is the consumer who must request the service. There is, though, a prohibition on restriction to the cross-border movement of essential personnel. It is limited in comparison to what the European Union envisages as a single financial market. The agreement did not introduce significant additional trade liberalisation between the United States and Canada that was not already contained in the 1989 bilateral Free Trade Agreement and was an attempt to liberalise and deregulate the previously highly regulated financial services market in Mexico.

The purpose of the General Agreement on Trade in Services, derived from the Uruguay Round of negotiations of the General Agreement on Tariffs and Trade, is to improve access to foreign markets, increase the volume of services provided cross-border, allow more services to be supplied and reduce restrictions on the type of foreign establishment. Services include financial services. The principles of the agreement are based on the most-favoured-nation principle and *de jure* national treatment.

The scope of the agreement is contained in three parts. Part I, Article I applies to trade in services and is defined as the supply of a service from the territory of one member country into that of another member country, from the territory of another member country to a customer in any other member country, or by a service provider of one member country through an office or through the presence of personnel in any other member country. The most-favoured-nation principle as outlined in Part II, Article II, means that each member country treats no less favourably services and service providers of any member country than it accords to like services and service providers of any other country.

Market access is outlined in Part III, Article XVI. Where a country allows a trade in a service and part of that service includes a cross-border movement of capital, the essential movement of capital may not be prohibited. This also applies to transaction involving offices established in another country. Restrictions on the total number of service providers, the total value of transactions or assets, the total number of offices or volume of output or the total number of expatriate personnel are prohibited where market access is allowed.

There are four modes of market access specified. These are cross-border supply of services, consumption of the service in the country of the supplier, foreign direct investment and the presence of personnel abroad. Mode 1 refers to pure cross-border trade in a service where the supplier and the consumer of the service are in two different countries and it is the service that is transported. It may be delivered by electronic means or other telecommunications or through mail. Mode 2 service transactions occur when the consumer consumes the service in the country of the supplier. Mode 3 transactions are the supply of a service in the country of the consumer through a foreign direct investment in the country of the consumer and recognise that the foreign office may be necessary to supply the service. Mode 4 service transactions are provided through the presence of an individual whether on a temporary basis and not remunerated in the foreign country or on a temporary transfer on a remunerated basis. Mode 1 applies where the consumer and supplier are in different countries and Mode 2 where the supplier consumes the service in the country of the supplier. There is no foreign direct investment by the supplier. Modes 3 and 4 apply where there is a presence of personnel or a commercial presence in the country of the consumer and these recognise the role of foreign direct investment in trade.

The financial services allowed are specified in an annex to the agreement and are similar to those in the Second Banking Co-ordination Directive of the European Union. That is, the main services provided by commercial and investment banks are included in the agreements. This annex, agreed in 1997, also includes a statement on prudential regulation which allows a government to follow policies to ensure the protection of customers or the stability and integrity of its financial system. This is not meant to avoid complying with the agreement's principles of openness. Defining precisely prudential regulation and the issue of national treatment, which must be negotiated, are the main focus in the ongoing discussions on trade in banking services, along with issues associated with electronic commerce.

Concentration in domestic banking markets

The concentration of assets of the leading five banks, deposit-taking institutions, in selected countries is outlined in Table 3.1. Significantly Germany, where the three main universal banks have strong competition from the wholesale public banks, *Landesbanken* and the retail savings banks, *Sparkassen,* as well as the co-operative banks, which account for 28% of assets, had the lowest market concentration in 1998.[12] The United States, which had regulations preventing interstate banking until quite recently, and Italy which has a fragmented banking market also have low concentrations. The Netherlands and

Table 3.1 Concentration in Banking 2003
Selected Countries' Percentage

Country	Concentration*
Canada	87
Netherlands	84
Switzerland	80
Spain	55
France	45
Japan	42
United Kingdom	41
Italy	27
United States	24
Germany	22

* Leading five banks' assets as a percentage of all banks' assets
Source: Bank for International Settlements, Annual Report, 2004, Table VII.3, p. 131

Switzerland, two relatively small countries in terms of population and area whose respective markets are dominated by two main banks following mergers, and Spain also, following consolidation leading to three main banks, have the highest concentrations. Canada has the highest concentration and although it has a larger population than the other highly concentrated countries it has had a banking market dominated by five large banks for a long period. Indeed, there were proposed separate mergers among four of these five banks in the late 1990s to reduce the number of banks to three and these were refused by the government.

As the data is based on the leading five banks' share of total assets the relatively lower populated countries, with consolidated banking markets dominated by a few large banks, such as the four highest ranked countries, would tend to have higher concentration ratios. Among the selected countries those that have less than 35 million in population have concentration ratios of 55 and above and the other countries with more than 60 million in population have concentration ratios of 45 and below. This suggests that relatively lower populated countries may be a stimulus for consolidation in banking markets as they may only be capable of sustaining a few large banks. This, of course, produces higher concentration ratios when measuring by such a criterion as the leading five banks' assets as a percentage of all banks' assets. The relatively lower population and higher concentration may be motivating factors for banks from these countries to be more internationally focused.

Cross-border mergers and acquisitions among financial firms

Between the ratification of the Single European Act in 1987 and the implementation of the single European market in 1993 there were 247 cross-border alliances in banking and financial services in the European Union by European Union banks. The largest number, 74, were by French banks targeting banks primarily in Spain, 19, the United Kingdom, 18, and Italy 10. British banks targeted 36 banks mostly in Italy, 9, France, 7, and Spain, 6, while German banks targeted 35 banks, the majority of which were in France, 10 and Spain, 9. Spanish and Italian banks targeted 33, 7 of which were French and 27 banks, 10 of which were French, respectively, and Dutch banks targeted 24 banks, evenly spread between member states. The data for initiating banks' and target banks' member states is outlined in Table 3.2.

The most common type of alliance was the purchase of a holding in small banks by larger banks which had a dominant position in their domestic market. Outright acquisitions accounted for 46%, minority stakes for 32%, share exchanges for 14%, and joint ventures for 8% of the activity. British and German banks favoured purchasing entirely or majority holdings. These accounted for 53% of British banks' alliances and 60% of German banks' alliances. French and Italian banks preferred minority holdings and these accounted for 39% of French banks' alliances and 44% of Italian banks' alliances. Spanish banks preferred share exchanges accounting for 55% of their alliances. Investment banks were mostly targeted in the United Kingdom.[13]

The data suggests that there could have been a regionalisation policy within the European Union being pursued by banks. The nature of the alliances also illustrates a somewhat hesitancy on the part of the banks to commit to what was probably perceived by them as an evolutionary and, as yet, untested single market as the majority of the alliances are not outright acquisitions. They may merely have been extending their market reach through non-acquisition alliances or extending the scope of their correspondent relationships.

There have also been some notable cross-border mergers and acquisitions in the European Union in particular the establishment of Dexia in 1996, and the emergence of Fortis in 1999 from five banks, two from Belgium and three Dutch banks. Another bank formed through cross-border mergers and acquisitions is Nordea bank following the mergers of four Nordic banks, commencing in 1997 with the merger between the Swedish bank Nordbanken and the Finnish bank Merita and this merged bank later merging in 2000 with the Danish bank Unidanmark and then

Table 3.2 Cross-Border Alliances in Banking and Financial Services in the European Union 1987–1993
Selected Countries

	Target Bank's Member State							
Targeting Bank's Member State	**F**	**D**	**I**	**NL**	**S**	**UK**	**Other**	**Total**
F	–	6	10	2	19	18	19	74
D	10	–	5	2	9	5	4	35
I	10	4	–	0	8	3	2	27
NL	5	2	1	–	4	5	7	24
S	7	6	3	2	–	4	11	33
UK	7	4	9	2	6	–	8	36
Other	5	0	0	2	3	4	4	18
Total	44	22	28	10	49	39	55	247

F = France, D = Germany, I = Italy, NL = Netherlands, S = Spain, UK = United Kingdom
Source: compiled from Bank of England, Cross-border Alliances in Banking and Financial Services in the Single Market, Quarterly Bulletin, August 1993, p. 374

acquiring the Norwegian bank Kreditkassen. The acquisition by HSBC of the United Kingdom of Crédit Commercial de France in 2000 and the acquisition by ING of the Netherlands of Banque Bruxelles Lambert were other significant cross-border acquisitions, along with Dresdner Bank's purchase of the investment bank Kleinworth Benson and Swiss Bank Corporation's acquisition of Warburg in 1995. BSCH of Spain acquired Abbey of the United Kingdom in 2005.

In the United States in 1980 there were 14,769 commercial banks and this declined to 8,704 by 1998. The average number of bank mergers and acquisitions in the United States was 345 per year between 1980 and 1989 increasing to 510 per year between 1990 and 1998. There were only 5,417 commercial banks, 62% of the total number of commercial banks, with assets less than $50 million in 1998 whereas in 1980 there were 10,799 banks, 73% of the total, in the same category, adjusted for inflation.[14]

Some large mergers and acquisitions in the United States were those of Bank America Corporation and Security Pacific Corporation in 1991, Chemical Bank's acquisition of Chase Manhattan in 1996, and the mergers between Bank America Corporation and NationsBank Corporation in 1998 and J.P. Morgan and Chase in 2001, as well as the merger between Citicorp and Travelers, an insurance firm, in 1998. Bank of America acquired FleetBoston in 2003 and JPMorgan Chase acquired Bank One in 2004.

Banks in the United States with less than $1 billion in assets have declined in number from more than 11,000 in 1984 to 6,000 in 2003. This category of bank represents a decline from 23% market share of total bank assets to 13% in that period. Medium sized banks, those with assets of between $ 1 billion and $ 25 billion, have also declined from 35% market share to 16% market share in the same period. Banks with assets of $25 billion or more have increased their share of total bank assets from 42% to 71%. There are several factors that led to the decline in market share. The elimination of restrictions on branching, allowing banks to enter other areas, and on interest rate limits led to more competition. Banks are also competing through the use of technology thereby extending market reach. Mergers and acquisitions among banks have also shifted these banks into a larger size category. In terms of profitability, measured by median return on assets for the different size of banks, large banks have increased profitability from almost 0.6% return on assets in 1984 to almost 1.4% in 2003. While the other categories of banks have also increased their return on assets the increase has not been as much. Banks with less than $1 billion in assets in 2003 had a median return of assets much the same as in 1984 at almost 1.1%. Medium sized banks' return on assets increased from 0.9% in 1984 to 1.3% in 2003.[15]

There have been over 5,500 mergers and acquisitions among banks in the Group of Ten countries, the majority between domestic banks.[16] Table 3.3 outlines the number and average value of these in selected countries between 1990 and 2001. These selected countries account for 95.5% of the total mergers and acquisitions in the Group of Ten countries.

The average value of the mergers and acquisitions is clustered around a quarter of a billion dollars. The most significant variations in the data are the low average value of bank mergers and acquisition in Canada, already a consolidated banking market before this period and dominated by five domestic banks, and the high average value in Japan, possibly due to the merger of Mitsubishi Bank and the Bank of Tokyo in 1996 and the establishment of Mizuho Bank in 2000. In all selected countries, except France, Italy and the Netherlands the majority of mergers and acquisitions during the period 1990–2001 were in the second half since 1996.

While the previous data related to banks only, the aggregate number of mergers between and acquisitions of commercial banks, securities

Table 3.3 Number and Value of Mergers and Acquisitions between Banks* 1990–2001
Selected Countries US Dollar Billions

Country	Number 1990–2001	Value	Average Value	Percentage of Total Number 1996–2001
France	244	56.4	.23	39
Germany	352	71.0	.20	65
Italy	285	99.6	.28	48
Netherlands	60	16.8	.28	40
United Kingdom	419	147.4	.35	67
United States	3,487	911.5	.26	52
Canada	164	16.6	.10	68
Japan	265	163.5	.62	89
Total G-10 countries	5,537	1,559.0	.28	55

* Deposit institutions and majority interests
Source: compiled from Amel, D., Barnes, C., De Long, G., and De Young, R., Consolidation and Efficiency in the Financial Sector: a Review of the International Evidence, Banca d'Italia, Temi di Discussione del Servizio Studi, Number 464, 2002, op. cit., Table 1, p. 10

firms and insurance firms from selected countries between 1985 and 2000 is outlined in Table 3.4 based on a study of cross-border mergers and acquisition of 1,859 banks, securities firms and insurance firms in 30 countries. There were 3,624 mergers and acquisitions among banks,

Table 3.4 Aggregate Number of Mergers and Acquisitions between Commercial Banks, Securities Firms and Insurance Firms 1985–2000
Selected Countries

	Domestic firm acquires domestic firm*	Domestic firm acquires foreign firm**	Foreign firm acquires domestic firm**
France	338	223	165
Germany	327	248	94
United Kingdom	1,143	451	488
United States	7,309	562	577
Japan	207	61	30

*Domestic for the European Union total and for the individual member states refers to mergers and acquisitions between firms within individual member state and between firms from other European Union member states
** Foreign for the European Union total and for the individual member states refers to mergers and acquisitions with firms from non-European Union countries
Source: compiled from Berger, A., Buch, C., De Long, G. and Young, R., Exporting Financial Institutions Management via Foreign Direct Investment Mergers and Acquisitions, Journal of International Money and Finance, 23, 2004, Table 1, p. 345.

securities firms and insurance firms in the European Union between 1985 and 2000, with almost 90% of these since 1990. Of the total there were 338, 327, 324, 137, 149 and 1,143 mergers and acquisitions alone between domestic firms, that is firms from within the European Union, in France, Germany, Italy, the Netherlands, Spain and the United Kingdom respectively. The data for foreign firms acquiring or merging with European Union firms reveals that consolidation has indeed been a feature of member states' financial markets.

Mergers and acquisitions between 1985 and 2000 between American financial firms, far outnumbered those between American and foreign firms. In the United States, the number peaked in 1997 and in the European Union in 1991. This was in line with the introduction of legislation, the Riegle-Neal Interstate Banking and Branching Efficiency Act in 1994 in the United States, allowing interstate banking and an initial response by firms to the abolishment of the restrictions, and the Second Banking Coordination Directive in the European Union in 1989, although there was resurgence of activity in the late 1990s in the European Union.[17]

Deregulation and harmonisation of banking markets, developments in technology that have reduced monitoring costs and globalisation of non-financial activity leading to a demand for international banking services are the three principal reasons for cross-border consolidation of banks according to Berger *et al.* Liberalisation of trade in banking services must, of course, also be added to these.

A method of measuring trade in banking services is based on the exports and imports of management through foreign direct investment. An export country is one whose financial firms have merged with or acquired a foreign financial firm and importing country is one whose financial firms have merged with or have been acquired by foreign financial firms.[18]

The countries with the largest export and import of management through foreign direct investment are France, Germany, the United Kingdom, the United States and Canada and the data on cross-border mergers and acquisitions between and among different types of financial firm from these selected countries between 1985 and 2000 is outlined in Table 3.5. Most of the countries seem balanced in terms of the number of exporting and importing mergers and acquisitions except Germany. The United Kingdom and the United States are 'net importers' in terms of the numbers of mergers and acquisitions with more foreign firms acquiring domestic firms than domestic firms merging with or acquiring foreign financial firms. This is similar to the data for the United Kingdom and the United States in Table 3.4.

The high proportion of acquisitions and mergers between financial firms within these selected countries suggests that financial firms have a preference for relatively larger countries with developed banking systems. Proximity and cultural similarities also seem to be motivating factors in the cross-border merger and acquisitions among financial firms.

The majority of acquisitions and mergers of foreign financial firms by British financial firms were in similarly linguistic countries, with firms from the United States accounting for 102, while there were also mergers and acquisitions among firms in other commonwealth countries such as Canada 19, Australia 35, and New Zealand 15. The other main group of countries targeted were in continental Europe, with 27 mergers and acquisitions among firms from France and 16 from Germany.

Table 3.5 Financial Firms' Cross-border Mergers and Acquisitions 1985–2000 Selected Countries Number and Percentage of Selected Countries' Total

	Importing country						
Exporting country	France	Germany	United Kingdom	United States	Canada	of which percentage of total	Country's Total Exports
France	0	10	35	26	2	49	154
Germany	27	0	28	29	0	48	182
United Kingdom	27	16	0	102	19	53	307
United States	18	10	152	0	62	66	365
Canada	2	0	17	86	0	89	118
of which percentage of total	55	47	66	60	91		
Country's Total Imports	135	76	352	407	98		

Source: compiled from Berger, A., Buch, C., De Long, G., and De Young R., Exporting Financial Institutions Management via Foreign Direct Investment Mergers and Acquisitions, Journal of International Money and Finance, 23, 2004, Table 2, p. 345.

The countries of origin of firms merging with or acquiring British firms were similar with 152 from the United States and 17 from Canada along with 18 from Australia, while among European countries there were 35 from France, 28 from Germany, 27 from Switzerland and 22 from the Netherlands. Financial firms from continental Europe concentrated mostly on merging and acquiring with other European financial firms. French firms merged with or acquired 35 British, 14 Belgian, 12 Spanish, 10 German, and 10 Swiss financial firms, and French financial firms were acquired by 27 British, 27 German, 17 Italian, 12 Dutch, and 11 Belgian financial firms. They also acquired 26 American financial firms and were acquired by 18 American firms. German firms merged with or acquired 28 British, 27 French, 15 Italian and 15 Dutch, 12 Swiss and 29 American financial firms and merged with or were acquired by 16 British, 11 Swiss, 10 French, and 10 American financial firms. American financial firms' mergers and acquisitions were mostly in the Group of Ten countries with 62 in Canada, 152 in the United Kingdom, 18 in France, 12 in Japan, 11 in Italy, 10 in Germany, and 28 in Australia. It is interesting that American firms acquired 14 Mexican firms but only two Mexican firms acquired American firms. This is in contrast with activity between American and Canadian financial firms. American financial firms merged with or were acquired by 86 Canadian firms, 102 British, 40 Swiss, 37 Dutch, 28 Japanese, 29 German and 26 French financial firms.

Significantly, Japan has a low volume of mergers and acquisitions among financial firms with only 43 exports and 20 imports, a net exporter, and Tokyo, unlike New York and London, which probably account for net imports in these countries, does not have the same pull on financial firms. Mergers and acquisitions between the same types of firm dominate with a minority of mergers and acquisitions between different types of institutions.

Cross-border mergers and acquisitions by banks targeting banks in emerging market economies increased from approximately $6 billion in value between 1990 and 1996 to almost $50 billion between 1997 and 2000. By far the largest number and value of this foreign direct investment was in Latin America followed by central and eastern Europe and non-Japan east Asia. Mexico, Brazil, Poland, South Korea, Argentina and the Czech Republic being the most frequent countries whose banks were targeted. Between 1990 and 2003 the value of cross-border mergers with and acquisitions of banks in Latin America as a target region was $46 billion, 56% of the total with emerging market economies, with Mexico alone accounting for 50% of this, primarily due to the acquisition of Banamex by Citigroup and Bancomer by BBVA. Central and Eastern Europe account for $20 billion in direct investment, that is, 24% of the total, and non-Japan East Asia for $14 billion or 17% of the total. In Latin America the main sources of foreign direct investment were banks from Spain and the United States accounting for 46% and 35% respectively of the value of cross-border mergers and acquisitions in banking. Banks from five European countries account for 70% of cross-border mergers and acquisitions with central and eastern European banks, and in terms of value these were Austrian banks which accounted for 18%, Italian banks which also accounted for 18%, Belgian banks which accounted for 13%, French banks which accounted for 11% and Danish banks which accounted for 10%. American banks dominated foreign direct investment in east Asia with 43% of the total value of cross-border mergers and acquisitions of banks in this target region, along with British banks 19% and Dutch banks 17%.

The main reason cited by banks for these direct investments were the potential and perceived profitability, although many cited that the privatisation of banks in many countries was a motivating factor. In terms of the legal form of the foreign direct investment, control of the business was a strong determining factor to protect the investing bank's brand, with full or majority ownership the most favoured form.[19]

Despite these cross-border mergers with and acquisitions of foreign banks and foreign direct investment by banks, retail banking customers in most European countries prefer to bank with their own country's banks. Of course, many may not realise that it is foreign owned, especially if the name of the bank is maintained. They also do not want a few large pan-European banks to emerge. These are some of the responses to a survey commissioned by KPMG. Conducted in 2004 it surveyed 2,300 retail bank customers in 10 European countries, the Czech Republic, France, Germany, Italy, the Netherlands, Poland, Spain, Sweden, Switzerland and the United Kingdom. The countries where customers are most strongly against the emergence of pan-European banks 'super banks' were Germany where 74% of those surveyed were against, the United Kingdom where 67% were against, Switzerland with 57% and the Netherlands and the Czech Republic with 50% of customers against these type of banks. However, it is these countries that have produced some of the largest banks in the world, for instance, Deutsche Bank, HSBC, Royal Bank of Scotland, Barclays Bank,

United Bank of Switzerland, Credit Suisse and ABN AMRO. In the Czech Republic one of the largest banks is Komercni Banka, a subsidiary of the French Bank, Société Générale. Those countries where customers are most in favour of 'super banks' are Spain 48% in favour, Italy 45% in favour and France 35% in favour. In fact one of France's largest banks, Crédit Commercial de France, is a subsidiary of HSBC. In total among customers in the 10 countries 46% are against 'super banks' and 26% are for their emergence. Among those surveyed 53% prefer to bank with their own country's banks and 28% prefer to bank with foreign banks. Customers in the United Kingdom were 73% in favour of banking with domestic banks and the other highest responses for country loyalty among customers were those in the Netherlands at 71% and in Sweden 54%. The implications for banks' strategies is that a large proportion of customers do not want pan-European banks to emerge, although 68% support a single financial services market, and also would prefer to bank with domestic banks. [20]

This means that there is a branding issue for banks. The strategy of HSBC was to maintain the name CCF and accompany it with the HSBC logo. They also follow this strategy with bank acquisitions in other countries. However, in France it is to integrate CCF totally into HSBC in 2005 by re-branding the bank as HSBC, similar to the phased strategy it followed with the branding of the acquired Midland Bank. HSBC's tagline, the 'world's local bank' is translated into French and also incorporated into its branding.

The majority of customers among all respondents, 57%, are also content with the banking system in their country and this has implications for banks establishing in these countries *de novo* and attempting to obtain market share, although 60% stated that they would consider purchasing a banking product from a foreign bank. The majority of customers, 53% of those surveyed, have been customers of their current bank for more than 10 years with the proportion being 68% in France, the Netherlands, the United Kingdom and 67% in Sweden.

When European banks are surveyed as to their opinions of retail banking they consider a strong brand and its development, as well as, reputation as being more important than global networks for banks as a means of differentiation and maintaining customers. Marketing strategy and a broad range of products are also considered important, as well as, online transactions. In terms of the development of the retail banking sector the majority of banks consider that the further development of strong brands is the most important and more so than further bank consolidation and cross-border networks.

These were the responses of 56 banks in 26 countries in a survey conducted by The Banker and Henrion Ludlow Schmidt on the retail bank of the future. In terms of factors important for banks in retail banking and the development of retail banking 96% responded that brand reputation is important for banks, and 89% agree that developing strong brands is the future of the retail banking sector. In terms of consolidation 60% consider that global networks are important for retail banks and 85% of respondents agree that increased consolidation is a future development in retail banking with 64% agreeing that cross-border consolidation is a future development. A large proportion of banks, 70%, also agree that switching banks by customers is another possible development in retail banking.[21]

This survey, and that focused on customers by KPMG, suggest that customers' preferences on retail banking seem to differ from bankers' opinions on branding and cross-border consolidation and on customer retention. There seems to be significant differences between customers' preferred retail banking industry developments in terms of brand and consolidation and banks' opinions on the developments of retail banking cross-border consolidation and branding and also on the possible retention rates of their customers although the majority of customers in the KPMG survey were long-term customers.

Electronic banking

Retail and wholesale electronic banking has emerged in the last 10 years with the development of the internet and the World Wide Web. Internet, or online, banking is conducted through a closed network. Most banks provide internet banking to both individual and corporate customers. Proximity is no longer a guarantee of a deposit base and banking services may be marketed and supplied through internet banking. While banks have sometimes provided banking services by mail the internet has the capacity to allow customers to be proactive and to manage their accounts themselves. This requires few if any interactions, other than the initial establishment of the relationship, between the banker and customer. However, internet banking, except for specialist internet banks, is not a substitute by banks for networks of offices. It is an enhanced and added service to customers to complement the existing network of offices. While many banks thought that it would replace networks this has not been the outcome. What it has achieved though is relatively lower operating costs of transactions through self-management of accounts, especially on low value high volume accounts, while maintaining fee income levels. It has been transformed into a resource for and a diffuser of information to customers and also for marketing banks' products.

Cross-border e-banking is defined as transactional online banking products or services by a bank located in one country to customers resident in another country. Usually there are no geographic indicators of the country of origin of the bank other than the internet address that incorporates a country designation, though this is not always used in the address, there being a generic designation instead. Some indicators of targeting a particular country include the language, the currency quoted on the web site, the use of the internet domain name most frequently applied to that country and advertising e-banking services using different media in that foreign country.[22] There is a further complication in that a website may have a hyperlink to other websites so that the actual country of location of the bank may be indeterminable.

Most banks that have branch networks provide internet banking services as an augmented parallel service to an existing branch network, whereby the customer has a choice of conducting banking business through one or either, or both, of these distribution channels. Alternatively a bank that has no physical office or a network of offices and offers banking products and services electronically may be termed a virtual bank.

A licensed virtual bank may be established as an independent bank *de novo*, or as a separately capitalised subsidiary of an existing bank, or transforming an existing bank into a virtual bank or by establishing a trade-name virtual bank. In 2001 in the United States there were only nine independent virtual banks and 20 trade name virtual banks.[23]

Electronic banking reduces distance and increases competition for banks in remote and protected markets. Those banks, usually large banks, with the capital available to invest in technology have an advantage over other banks as one of the most important factors for banks when competing, especially through electronic banking, is ensuring the confidence of customers in the bank, an attribute of brand, image and reputation.

The leading banks in internet banking are outlined in Table 3.6. This ranking is based on criteria such as attracting and servicing online customers, range of products and the increase in the online customer base among others.

The leading internet bank in most countries is a domestic bank, especially for retail online banking. This is not unusual considering it is most often an additional service and not an alternative service. What is revealing is the extent of Citigroup's reach globally. In the category corporate and institutional internet banking it was the leading bank in 20 out of a total of 42 countries. Citigroup, along with Banamex in Mexico its wholly owned subsidiary, and JPMorgan Chase dominate corporate and institutional internet banking services in the categories of cash management and integrated site and securities research respectively. Citigroup is the leading internet bank in cash management in Europe, North America and Latin America, Asia-Pacific and Middle East and Africa. It was awarded the leading integrated site award in Europe, North America and Latin America. JPMorgan Chase was the leading bank in securities research in Europe, North America and Latin America.[24]

Personal electronic international banking, that is cross-border payments and settlements by personal customers using credit and debit cards, whether through the internet, by mail or by telephone, has accelerated, partly due to the increase in the number of credit and debit cards, but correspondingly also due to the spread of information

Table 3.6 Leading Banks in Retail and Corporate Internet Banking 2004 Selected Countries

Country	Corporate and Institutional	Retail
Netherlands	Citigroup	*
Spain	BBVA	BBVA
United Kingdom	Citigroup	*
United States	Citigroup	Wells Fargo
Canada	Scotia Capital	Toronto Dominion Trust
Mexico	Banamex	Banamex
Russia	Citigroup	*
China	Citigroup	*
Singapore	Citigroup	Citigroup
Australia	ANZ	*

* no award for retail internet banking in these countries
Source: Global Finance, The World's Best Internet Banks, September 2004

and communication technologies at lower costs and the accelerated adoption of these technologies by customers in a relatively short space of time. Many transactions that would have been settled through mail or telegraphic transfer through a bank and its correspondents are settled electronically directly by personal customers thereby reducing the fee income for banks. Indeed, foreign currency is also available in the home country as well as the currency of a country of location of the customer through distributors.

Part III

Internationally Traded Banking Services

4

Trade Theories and International Banking

International banking is comprised of cross-border banking services and foreign direct investment by banks. The choice of strategy determines the range of services that a bank may offer and depends on the resources of the bank. Banks may also provide cross-border banking services through foreign offices to its home country and to third countries. These strategies are not substitutes as much of what is considered cross-border banking requires a foreign presence to originate the business and to deliver the service. Another element to trade in banking services involves the temporary presence of bank personnel in a foreign country to transact business, whether through a permanent foreign office in that country or not.

Banks are multi-product firms. Therefore they may compete by cross-subsidising services, that is, by increasing the price of services with a low price elasticity of demand and reducing the price for other services to gain market share or to reduce the cost of production of those services.

In general, services cannot be stored as they must be produced and rendered at the same time and in the same place. These temporal and spatial aspects to a service means that it must be transported to the customer or the customer must move to where the producer is located.

In banking some services may be produced at a distance through the use of telecommunications technology, such as, screen based trading but the temporal element in this instance is not eliminated. Information and its exploitation is a core element for international service industries according to Hindley and Smith.[1] Information flows freely across borders among bank offices and between banks.

Firms, governments and non-governmental and supranational organisations have access to international money and capital markets with few restrictions and these are the main types of customers with whom banks transact business in international financial markets. Banks that establish offices abroad also usually transact with corporate customers and many are in niche markets of corporate banking, although some have acquired banks in foreign countries and thereby acquired retail banking networks. Most individual customers do not transact business in international markets and have a relatively lower demand than corporate customers for international banking services and which are mostly cross-border payments and settlements and foreign exchange, although these may be transacted with either indigenous or foreign banks in the customer's country.

While there is a strong relationship between cross-border trade in banking services and foreign direct investment by banks there are fundamental differences between international banks and multinational banks. A bank may be international without being multinational, depending on where its transactions are booked, the residency of the customer and the currency of the transaction. When a service is rendered and the transaction is booked in the country of the bank providing the service and where the customer is a non-resident the bank is only providing a cross-border service. By booking the transaction abroad, whether in the country of the customer or a third country, the bank is acting as a multinational bank.

The theories of international trade attempt to explain why firms, including banks, transact business internationally. The theories extend to cross-border trade, foreign direct investment and financial centres. Foreign direct investment is not a substitute for cross-border trade and several studies suggest that firms that invest directly abroad are important generators of cross-border trade. Foreign direct investment is also an important element in the increase in capital flows.

While there are barriers to trade in all industries, the banking industry is particularly characterised by barriers to trade and establishment, restrictions on the ownership of banks and the type of business permitted mostly due to the industry's role in economies. Furthermore, foreign direct investment is complementary to trade in banking services and often a necessary condition for providing many types of banking services. The theory of comparative advantage may be applied to trade in most service industries.[2]

Theories of international trade

The classical theories of absolute and comparative advantage explain the motives for international trade in goods and services in terms of variations in the cost of production between different countries and benefits to countries from trading. The theories focus on industries rather than firms. Adam Smith demonstrated that international trade based on specialising in the production of products with absolute cost advantages was beneficial to trading countries. Ricardo extended the theory introducing comparative advantage based on relative costs of production and conditions of free trade. This theory states that when countries agree to trade, even though one may have an absolute advantage, they gain through specialisation and more efficient production of products in which they have opportunity costs whenever these opportunity costs differ between the countries.

The neo-classical Heckscher-Ohlin theory, extended by Samuelson, explains international trade based on factor endowments and location-specific differences. It compares differences between industries within a country and not between the same industries in different countries. This theory, along with the classical theories, assumes that factors of production are immobile internationally. Foreign direct investment is not considered. It also assumes perfect competition in product and factor markets. There is no allowance for differences in the quality of personnel which is a major competitive advantage in service industries. It does not allow for imperfections in markets or economies. Comparative advantage based trade theories suggest that while countries benefit from trade, the trade patterns would tend to be between countries that differ in terms of factor endowments and location advantages. Arndt maintains that this theory is not very relevant to trade in banking services. Countries gained a comparative advantage in banking through domestic demand for such services and this in turn led to efficiency and a skilled labour force.[3]

The classical and neo-classical trade theories are based on internationally traded standardised products, without allowing for differences in service quality or in tastes among customers, and cannot explain intra-industry trade. Intra-industry trade relates to trade in products, including services, produced by firms in the same industry in different countries. Banking is an industry in which a high proportion of trade is intra-industry. The theory of intra-industry trade is based on an industrial organisation approach, emphasising monopolistic competition, economies of scale and scope, product differentiation, learning curve economies and innovation, as well as incorporating foreign direct investment into the theories, as reasons for intra-industry trade.

Theories based on economies of scale state that there are advantages to firms located in a country with a high demand for its products, provided that economies of scale are attainable by firms in the industry. Economies of scale occur when an increase in the volume of production is accompanied by a reduction in the unit cost of production. When scale economies exist in an industry it would tend to be made up of a few large firms. That is, relatively larger firms would have an advantage and would be a barrier to other firms, especially foreign firms, entering a market. With few restrictions on foreign direct investment or on the scope of business allowed there would tend to be mergers between or acquisitions of firms. Most banks emphasise the possible synergies to be gained as a motivating factor in a merger or an acquisition, though studies of economies of scale in banking seem to suggest that these are limited when banks become large. Economies of scale for banks may be achieved by spreading risk, by exploiting information through the use of technology, or by processing larger volumes of business.

Economies of scope exist when two or more products are produced together and the cost of production is lower than when they are produced separately. Intermediation where banks produce deposits and loans jointly provides commercial banks with economies of scope. The cost of production is lower than producing these services individually as the bank has sources of information that are proprietary and may not be traded. The lending of aggregate available deposits is more efficient than applying specific deposits to specific customers. Economies of scope may be achieved through sharing information and providing a wide range of products to different customer types and sectors throughout a bank's network. Banks have recently been complementing their range of products, such as investment products and non-banking products, such as insurance.

When markets are protected firms tend to be less efficient. The more competition there is the more efficient firms tend to be. Hanweck and Schull conclude that while there are possible economies of scale in banks with up to $1 billion in assets there may be diseconomies of scale in larger banks and that there is inconclusive support for economies of scope in banking. They also state that possible profit efficiencies, estimated to be between 24% and 67% of potential profits for the average bank, and possible cost efficiencies, estimated at between 21% and 30%, suggest that there is enormous potential for improving bank management. This suggests that the relative higher profits of large banks may be due to other factors other than to superior efficiency and that large banks should focus on improving efficiency.[4]

Contestable markets are characterised by low barriers to trade and investment and low entry and exit barriers. That is, sunk costs are almost non-existent thereby allowing firms to enter a market with or without a long-term commitment and to compete with local firms. A permanent commitment market exists when the exit costs are high and the entry costs are either high or low. Banking markets have historically been highly protected due to the pivotal role of banks in an economy and the externalities associated with the banking industry. Recently banking markets have been de-regulated and trade in banking services liberalised and banks are obliged to become more efficient with the increase in the number of banks establishing abroad. Competition between banks has produced dynamic gains, especially in the competition for corporate business. Openness of markets is a factor in the increase in the volume of intra-industry trade.

When firms establish abroad, as opposed to providing cross-border services through home offices, screen based trading or the temporary presence of personnel, they are engaging in foreign direct investment. One explanation of foreign direct investment is the ownership, location, internalisation paradigm developed by Dunning. The ownership advantages that firms, such as banks, possess include such intangible assets as proprietary knowledge, technology, management expertise in the form of human capital, and brand, especially when the firm produces complex knowledge or information based products. Other advantages are economies of scale and scope and access to inputs. Advantages must be firm-specific to be transferable and to sustain an advantage through distinctive competencies.

Location advantages consist of available personnel, government incentives and taxation policy, market regulations, infrastructure and access to markets. These advantages must outweigh the alternative of exporting. Whenever a firm considers it more beneficial to produce a product itself rather than licence it to other producers, or produce at all stages of the production process or transact between subsidiaries rather than interact with the market there is a strong argument to internalise production. Of course, firms may also want to internalise production to protect supply of inputs or product quality. Knowledge intensive firms, such as banks, may want to maintain proprietary information within the firm rather than transfer it to possible competitors with possibilities of knowledge spillover within the firm that it would prefer to exploit internally.

Theories of international banking

Arndt defines a country's exports of financial services as the products and services that are provided to non-residents.[5] Trade in financial services are distinguished from capital movements, factor incomes, foreign direct investment and international financial centres.

Services are contained in people, capital or information and these are rendered internationally when there is a movement of people or a flow of capital or a flow of information.[6]

The production and consumption of certain financial services, that are separated spatially and temporally, may be rendered at different levels according to Jones and Ruane. They distinguish between trade in the service factor and trade in the service product. They relate this to banking services whereby the banking factor comprises managerial and technical competencies and the banking product is the actual type of service the bank renders. Trade in the banking factor relates to foreign direct investment when a non-traded banking service is produced in combination with local banking factors. Trade in the banking product relates to cross-border trade in banking services when there is no further production process after the trade.[7]

Whenever a bank provides a service to non-resident customers they are engaging in a trade in an international service, as they are moving to the client to render the service, even when the service is rendered through a foreign office, as the initial movement was the establishment of the office abroad.[8]

A theory of international banking by Aliber is based on efficient banks in a free market having the possibility to pay higher rates on deposit and charge lower rates on loans, effectively operating with a lower net margin. Applying this argument to free trade in banking services, efficient banks would eliminate differences in spreads between countries as customers should choose banks with the better rates. Less efficient banks would have to compete on price to maintain market share thereby reducing profits. Eventually the more efficient banks would increase capital and market share accelerating the consolidation process in financial markets.[9] This, however, does not incorporate the segmented nature of financial markets, the information of local banks, loyalty and switching costs of customers, reputation of bank and that the foreign bank may attract the least creditworthy customers.

The eclectic theory of international production based on ownership-specific advantages, location-specific advantages and internalisation advantages is applied to multinational banks by Gray and

Gray.[10] They differentiate between supranational, or offshore banking, and national banking markets. They assume that multinational banks have ownership-specific advantages and consider these a prerequisite for internalisation and in their analysis they apply location-specific and internalisation advantages that include production techniques, innovation, management efficiency and integration of technology. They considered three types of advantages in each of the location-specific and internalisation advantages categories. These are imperfections in markets, imperfections in factor or input markets, economies of internal production, preservation of established customer accounts, that is, market share, entry into a growing or high growth market and control over a raw material source. They concluded that access to global markets is more advantageous for multinational banks than non-multinational banks, though not a significant advantage. Information is a clear advantage when following customers abroad and an important incentive to establish foreign offices and also provides opportunities for additional business from existing customers and new customers. Sourcing funds is also an important incentive to establish abroad and internal production reduces cost, such as, internal funds management.

An internalisation approach to the theory of multinational banking, whereby a bank may transfer abroad a monopolistic advantage, is considered by Casson.[11] This theory focuses on why banks internalise rather than transact with the market. The main reason is due to transaction costs and internalisation economies alone are an advantage. The size of the country of origin is a strong determinant of international trade in banking services, according to a study by Ter Wengel, and supports the theory of economies of scale as an explanatory factor for international trade in banking services.[12]

Having access to resources is only part of the source of competitive advantage. Some of the inputs that are important in providing banks with a competitive advantage are capital, personnel and delivery channels. Technology is another input and as the cost of technology declines then large banks' advantages are diluted. This is especially relevant in the provision of technology based banking services, such as internet banking for individual and corporate customers and for marketing services.

Superior capability to manage and organise resources to obtain distinctive competencies along with access to inputs at a lower cost and also efficient cost management, learning effects and economies of scale and scope provide banks with sources of competitive advantage.

A supply of inputs at a lower cost than competitor banks is only an advantage when the bank is capable of managing and organising these resources effectively and efficiently.

Berger *et al* conclude that developed economies are more likely to engage in intra-industry trade through the export of management in their foreign direct investments and that similarity in culture, language, legal systems and economic size and development, as well as, geographic proximity are positive factors in cross-border mergers and acquisitions between financial firms.[13]

As trade in goods and services increases exports of banking services decline, that is cross-border trade in banking services, such that banks tend to engage more in foreign direct investment and also tend to establish their foreign offices in countries with high sovereign credit ratings rather than export banking services.[14]

Foreign direct investment is a significant contributory factor in intra-industry trade in insurance services and multinational insurance firms also generate trade in insurance services. Some other determinants in intra-industry trade in insurance services are differences in per capita income and differences in financial market size and market openness.[15]

The level of development of the financial sector and legal systems and the level of foreign direct investment by firms, financial and non-financial, are factors in the foreign direct investment decisions of banks. There are wide variations in the share of banking assets held by foreign controlled banks in a study of 91 countries in 1998. The countries with more than a 10% share are developing and emerging economies or those in transition, with the exception of Spain at 11%, Australia at 17.1%, Luxembourg at 95% and New Zealand at 99%. Conversely, there are several developing countries with less than 5% foreign controlled share of banking assets. This study also outlines the share in relation to the level of foreign direct investment, the development of the domestic financial system and the legal system. In countries with a developed legal system and an underdeveloped financial system the share was 26.4%. In countries where the level of foreign direct investment is high the share of banking assets held by foreign controlled banks is 44% when the domestic financial system is underdeveloped, and only 18.2% in those countries with a relatively developed financial system.[16]

There are three central reasons for the internationalisation of banking according to Bryant.[17] These are financial activity following real sector activity, consisting of payments services, financial activity leading real sector activity, consisting of banks establishing foreign offices, not specifically to provide services to existing customers but, due to advances in communications technology, to provide banking services to other customers and also to provide a broader range of services other than payments services, and to avoid regulation and tax.

A survey in 1996, before the introduction of the Euro, of 1,129 firms relating to credit activities and non-credit cash management services of their affiliates in 20 countries in Europe, whose head office may be in any country including outside Europe, yielded data on 2,118 affiliates in these countries. There were 255 different banks in total that supplied banking services to these affiliates. These banks are categorised as a home country bank when the location of the bank's head office is the same as the location of the affiliate's head office, a host country bank when the location of the affiliate and the bank's head office differ and the bank is from the same country as the location of the affiliate, and a third country bank when the location of the bank's head office is in another country other than the affiliate and the bank providing the service. Banks' subsidiaries are assumed to have the same nationality as the owning banks' head offices when they are majority controlled. The data for 15 European Union member states and Norway and Switzerland are outlined in Table 4.1. These account for 1,977 or 93% of the affiliates surveyed.

Table 4.1 Banking Services in Europe to Affiliates of Foreign Firms

	Number of Affiliates	Host Country Bank Percentage	Home Country Bank Percentage	Third Country Bank Percentage
Classified by Location of Affiliate				
Large Banking Sector 7*	1,201	69.1	17.9	13.0
Small Banking Sector 10**	776	67.0	14.8	18.2
Classified by Country of Origin of Affiliate				
Large Banking Sector7*	892	69.3	10.8	20.0
Small Banking Sector 10**	716	70.9	11.5	17.6
United States	470	49.1	41.7	9.1
Canada	22	72.7	0.0	27.3
Japan	9	77.8	0.0	22.2

* France, Germany, Italy, Netherlands, Spain, United Kingdom and Switzerland.
** Austria, Belgium, Denmark, Finland, Greece, Ireland, Luxembourg, Portugal, Sweden and Norway.
Source: Berger, A., Dai, Q., Ongena, S. and Smith D., To What Extent will the Banking Industry be Globalised? A Study of Bank Nationality and Reach in 20 European Nations, Journal of Banking and Finance, 27, 2003, Table 2, p. 392 and Table 3, p. 393

There is a strong bias towards to host country banks. This 'concierge effect' suggests that there is a preference for banks that have local knowledge. There are variations between the individual banking sector countries though. Among the large banking sector countries the range varies from 52.2% in the United Kingdom to 78.3% in the Netherlands and among the small banking sector countries the range varies from 15% in Luxembourg to 85.3% in Sweden. When the affiliates are classified by country of origin the responses are much the same. The choice of bank is predominantly a host country bank. This data suggests that there is a limited scope for providing banking services by following customers abroad.[18]

There is some support for this based on rankings of banks in treasury and cash management services. Those considered the best by region are outlined in Table 4.2. There are 34 countries represented by the four regions. There are only six banks that are considered the best bank in these regions. There are four European banks, Deutsche Bank, HSBC, BSCH and ABN-AMRO, and two American Banks Citigroup and JPMorgan Chase.

Europe is dominated by European banks as is North America by North American banks. Latin America is dominated by Citigroup and BSCH, an American and Spanish bank respectively, both of which have significant direct investments in the region. HSBC dominates in Asia where it is widely represented and which is its original region of business.

Table 4.2 Best Treasury and Cash Management Banks 2004

Region	Cash Management	Liquidity and Working Capital Management	Money Market Funds	Risk Management	Cross-Border Pooling and Netting	Payments and Collections
Europe	Deutsche Bank	Deutsche Bank	Citigroup	United Bank of Switzerland	ABN AMRO	Deutsche Bank
North America	Citigroup	Citigroup	Citigroup	JPMorgan Chase	JPMorgan Chase	JPMorgan Chase
Latin America	BSCH	Citigroup	BSCH	BSCH	Citigroup	Citigroup
Asia	HSBC	HSBC	HSBC	HSBC	Citigroup	HSBC

Source: Best Treasury and Cash Management Banks and Providers, World's Best Banks, Global Finance, January 2005

Banking is an information based industry and banks develop relationships with and obtain information on their customers. Following them abroad, therefore, is a motivating factor for banks to continue providing banking services and also for defensive reasons. Besides this follow-the-client factor there may also be an incentive to establish abroad to circumvent regulation, such as, establishing offices in offshore financial centres. The size and opportunities of potentially larger foreign markets, providing a higher return on capital, higher net interest margins and higher fee income also motivate banks to invest directly abroad, reinforced by possible lower competition and lower cost of capital. Of course, banks may have to extend geographic scope due to few opportunities in their domestic market.

There were 67 Italian banks with foreign offices in 1999 and 39 of these had representative offices only while 19 had had both representative offices and branches and nine had branches only. There were 95 branches in total among these banks. The distribution of these were 49 in Europe with 17 of these in the United Kingdom, 15 in the United States and 16 in Asia, with seven in Singapore, six in Hong Kong and three in Japan. Though Italian banks have weak ownership advantages partly due to the scale and concentration of its domestic banking market and the relatively lower level of internationalisation by its non-bank industries they tend to maintain their relationships with whatever firms have internationalised. International financial centres are also a strong indicator of Italian bank presence.[19]

Liberalisation, international trade agreements and reduced trade barriers and more open markets have allowed banks to expand internationally. Banks, though, must have some distinctive competencies to have a competitive advantage in competing with indigenous banks when they invest directly abroad.

International financial centres

Financial centres consist of clusters of financial services firms, as well as, firms from complementary and supporting industries, that benefit from external economies of scale, agglomeration effects and input specialisation. Another feature of clusters is the knowledge spillovers between firms in the same industry and between similar firms in related and supporting industries.

Throughout the pre-modern and modern banking eras political stability, developed legal and regulatory systems and available capital have been the basis for the emergence of financial centres. In the contemporary banking era developed telecommunications and infrastructure, a broad range of complementary and supporting services, broad and deep financial markets with related financial institutions and financial products, and confidence in the political establishment and regulatory authorities are the basis for the viability of financial centres. Innovation in products and processes and also in regulation is the means for sustaining the advantages of financial centres.

London, New York and Tokyo may be considered as the leading international and, indeed global, financial centres, such as Amsterdam was in the then trading world of the 17th and 18th centuries, as well as being the principal financial centre in their respective regions. There are also other financial centres in these regions, and while they are international in their activities they do not have the breadth and depth of the markets of the global financial centres. Offshore financial centres differ in that they are in many instances tax havens or booking centres or preferential tax regimes. These are by definition also international due to the type of business activities that is conducted and the international flow of funds through these centres.

Financial centres developed in specific locations, much the same as trade fairs did, in centres of trading and at strategic locations on trade routes and also decline in importance for much the same reasons as trade fairs did. They developed in centres in the premodern era where there were trade fairs and where foreign traders and bankers were protected by law or by custom. Bankers provided services in the form of money exchange and credit. The decline of these centres was due to political instability, war or the withdrawal of support and protection to foreigners.

Amsterdam emerged following political instability in Antwerp and was also the centre of the then world multilateral payments system. Amsterdam was the leading trading port and the United Provinces the leading trading nation. Capital was available and all the institutions usually associated with a financial centre were established there. London emerged for similar reasons, war and political instability in Amsterdam and the rise of the United Kingdom as the leading trading country. In the 19th century there was rivalry between London and other continental European financial centres. Eventually war and revolution were to weaken this rivalry in continental Europe. New York emerged due to the effects of World War I on the United Kingdom and was the leading world financial centre in the inter-war period. London re-emerged in the late 1950s as the main rival to New York due to regulations in the United States on certain financial activities and the development of the euromarkets. Tokyo became the most important financial centre in Asia and also a leading international financial centre as Japan was the leading Asian trading country in the post-World War II period. Tokyo only became the leading national financial centre in the 1960s and its development paralleled the rapid economic development and international trade of the country.

In Europe Paris, Frankfurt, Milan, Zurich and Madrid are regional financial centres with London as the leading international financial centre. In North America New York is the leading international financial centre with regional centres in Chicago and San Francisco and also in Toronto and Montréal. Other regional centres in Asia and Oceania are Hong Kong, Singapore, Shanghai and Sydney. With advances in telecommunications there is also a location advantage. In terms of trading New York's markets' opening hours overlap with those of San Francisco and also with Chicago and London. London markets overlap with those of Paris and Frankfurt and also with the Middle Eastern countries. Tokyo, Singapore and Hong Kong also overlap in market opening hours.

Financial centres are characterised by the availability of large volumes of capital for investment, the clearing of financial transactions, the clustering of expertise and complementary services, the broad range of financial institutions and the personnel that is available to provide the banking services that are located in the centre. To emerge as an international financial centre there must be a willingness for international investment of capital and the expertise and infrastructure to support the international business activities.

Taxation is a factor in the emergence and competitiveness of offshore financial centres and this fiscal regime is the basis for their competition as well, of course, as the regulatory factors. Usually there is no business interaction between banks located in these centres and the domestic economy and essentially the international banking element is sealed from domestic banking. There are also supranational financial centres though these are in effect wholesale offshore markets that consist of networks of banks operating in an unregulated though insulated market without a specific location and interacting through telecommunications.

In a study to determine the most important factors for an international financial centre academics and practitioners were surveyed. The ranking in importance of the criteria they consider important for establishing in a financial centre and the factors they consider for London being the leading financial centre in Europe are outlined in

Table 4.3. There are some notable differences between academics and financial journalists and banks, investment firms and financial consultancies. These groups agree on seven of the 10 criteria though in a different order. The practitioners consider an historical financial culture, the circulation of information and the banking sector in the centre to

Table 4.3 The Most Important Criteria for a Financial Centre and Factors for the Leadership of London in Europe

Academics, Financial Journalists, Researchers	Banks, Investment Firms and Financial Consultancies	Academics, Banks, Investment Firms, Financial Consultancies, Exchanges and Central Banks Composite	Factors for London as Leading Centre in Europe
Availability of Capital	Human Resources	Human Resources	Human Resources
Diversity and Size of Markets	Diversity and Size of Markets	Diversity and Size of Markets	Historical Financial Culture
Human Resources	Diversity of Financial Products	Diversity of Financial Products	Diversity and Size of Markets
Other International Banks in Centre	Other International Banks in Centre	Other International Banks in Centre	Other International Banks in Centre
Diversity of Financial Products	Historical Financial Culture	Volume of Transactions	Diversity of Financial Products
Market Regulation	Circulation of Information	Market Regulation	Market Regulation
Volume of Transactions	Market Regulation	Infrastructure	Banking Sector
Operating Costs	Infrastructure	Operating Costs	Innovation
Settlement of Transactions	Volume of Transactions	Availability of Capital	Availability of Capital
Infrastructure	Banking Sector	Historical Financial Culture	Language

Source: Bindemann, K., The Future of European Financial Centres, Routledge, London, 1999, pp. 28–30

be of importance and the academics and journalists consider availability of capital as the most important and also operating costs and settlement of transactions. The aggregate of the criteria considered the most important by different groups for an international financial centre when establishing there are similar to the factors for London's leadership among European financial centres. There are seven factors in common with the aggregate responses and also with the banks, investment firms and financial consultancies group's criteria. There are only six factors in common with the academics and journalists group's criteria. Interestingly the practitioners do not rank operating costs and the academics and journalists do not rank historical financial culture and circulation of information and neither of these groups rank innovation among their 10 most important criteria for an international centre.

The availability of personnel, the number of international banks in the centre, the supply and cost of funds, the size of the markets, regulation, infrastructure, telecommunications, settlement systems, time zone, taxation and operating cost are the most important criteria for financial centres. The leading international financial centres are also located in countries whose currencies are the leading trading currencies.

An analysis of foreign banks in London and New York illustrates the number and the type of office that these banks establish. There are 242 foreign owned banks in London. In New York there are 218 foreign owned banks. The origin of these banks is diverse. There are banks from 63 different countries in London and from 56 different countries in New York. The majority of foreign banks in London and New York originate from Europe. The European Union, North America and Japan account for almost half the foreign banks in London and more than half the banks in New York, as outlined in Table 4.4.

Table 4.4 Foreign Banks in London 2004 and New York 2003

Origin	London Number of Banks	New York Number of Banks
European Union	81	81
Other Europe	24	12
United States and Canada	19	6
Japan	16	28
Other Asia	54	55
Other Countries	48	36
Total	242	218

Source: The Banker, Foreign Banks in New York, May, 2003, and Foreign Banks in London, November, 2004

The largest component of operating expenses for a bank comprises personnel expenses and premises. The salary levels and the prime office rental charges for the leading international and regional financial centres are outlined in Table 4.5. As the number of personnel increases so does the personnel expense and also the office space required. Therefore the expense of locating in certain financial centres is a constraint on the range of activities of foreign banks in these centres, the volume of core business activity and the number of personnel.

Tokyo and London are the most expensive with New York slightly ahead of Paris and Frankfurt. In terms of personnel expenses New York and Tokyo are the most expensive and London and Tokyo are the most expensive for office occupancy. While the leading banks are represented in the leading international financial centres and these are also regional financial hub centres the three centres in Europe are in competition to attract foreign banks and certain banking activities. Frankfurt and Paris have an advantage in that it is less expensive for banks to establish offices in these cities which are relatively close and easily accessible to London. New York has an advantage over the other international financial centres where the personnel expenses and the office occupancy expenses are 84% of London's and 80% of Tokyo's.

The business activities of foreign banks in London are outlined in Table 4.6 for selected countries. These countries' banks are among the leading banks and would be represented in the leading international financial centres and most regional financial centres. These countries'

Table 4.5 Personnel and Office Occupancy Expenses in Financial Centres 2004

	Personnel Expenses Index*	Office Occupancy Expenses Index**	Composite Index
London City	100.0	100.0	200.0
Paris	82.1	70.1	152.2
Frankfurt	94.3	49.3	143.6
New York Mid Town	123.6	43.6	167.2
Tokyo Inner Central	110.6	97.3	207.9
London = 100			

* Personnel expenses index is based on the gross income in various industries in the selected cities.

** Office occupancy expenses include rent and other expenses in commercial areas.

Source: United Bank of Switzerland, Prices and Earnings, 2003 and Richard Ellis Incorporated, 2004

Table 4.6 Foreign Banks' Business Activities in London 2004 Selected Countries and Number of Banks by Business Activity

Origin	Total Number of Banks	Business Activity										
		Corporate Lending	Foreign Exchange	Trade Finance	Securities Dealing	Personal Lending	Private Banking	Risk Management	Mergers and Acquisitions	Trust and Investment Management	Global Custody	Leasing
European Union and Switzerland	81	69	56	46	32	14	22	20	28	10	8	10
United States and Canada	19	13	17	10	11	2	6	8	6	7	7	4
Japan	16	9	7	4	6	1	0	2	0	1	4	1
Other	126	63	67	70	23	42	29	17	6	14	3	6
Total Number of Banks	242	154	147	130	72	69	57	47	40	32	22	21

Source: compiled from The Banker, Foreign Banks in London, November, 2004

banks also represent 47 of the 56 banks ranked among the leading 50 by assets or Tier 1 capital. They represent the main activities of banks in financial centres. The main banking activities of the 242 foreign banks in London are also outlined.

It is clear from the data on assets, as outlined in Table 4.7, that foreign banks with offices in New York are focused on the New York market and have a market share of more than 50% compared to the United States in total where foreign banks have only a 17.8% market share. In terms of lending they also specialise in business loans in both the New York market, where they have a dominant share and the total United States market. There is a significant proportion of domestic loans held by foreign banks in New York. However, total loans are only 21.3% of total assets of foreign banks in New York and only 30.5% nationally. Total assets of foreign banks in New York are almost 70% of total assets of all foreign banks in the United States.

A recent phenomenon is the offshoring of financial services firms' support services, that is, the production of labour intensive processing functions in relatively lower cost labour markets. There was a 46% increase in 2003 in the number of financial institutions that have offshore activities, an increase of 500% in employment in offshore operations. More than 80% of financial institutions with market capitalisation of $10 billion or more have offshore operations. It is estimated that by end 2005 the amount of the largest 100 financial institutions' production cost base located in offshore operations could be as much as $210 billion resulting in efficiencies in these institutions of $71 billion.[20]

Table 4.7 Selected Domestic Assets of New York Offices of Foreign Banks* 2004
US Dollar Billions and Percentage Share of Market as at Third Quarter

	Total Loans	Total Business Loans	Total Assets
Branches and Agencies	210.0	109.8	1,006.7
Subsidiaries	13.4	5.9	41.0
Total Foreign New York	223.3	115.7	1,047.7
Percentage Share	32.8	64.3	52.6
Total Foreign National	461.3	185.8	1,512.0
Percentage Share	9.8	20.8	17.8

* Foreign bank offices in the United States, United States' commercial banks of which more than 25% is owned by foreign banks and International Banking Facilities
Source: compiled from Federal Reserve Board of Governors, Structure and Share Data of U.S. Offices of Foreign Banks, Statistical Release, December 2004

Captive offshoring is foreign direct investment and differs from outsourcing in a foreign country in that the offshoring firm establishes its own operations abroad and internalises its activities. Technological advances have reduced distance in the sense that it allows production in locations that are farther from the centre. This type of bank foreign direct investment is different in that it is primarily to produce support services similar to what would have been previously produced in its home country and also in that the purpose of other types of bank foreign direct investment is to provide banking services, its principal activity, and to participate in foreign financial markets. Essentially is it a dislocation and not an extension of banking market or product reach.

For banks the most common types of captive offshoring is in low value added back-office processing, call centres and customer services. However, some other high value added middle office functions activities, such as finance and information technology, are also being offshored as many banks are creating shared service centres. Typically these support services are highly technical with standardised procedures. While many of the activities that are transferred offshore are low skill level production of support services, others require professionally qualified and highly competent personnel. The ease of relocation of technical support services such as information technology and finance lend themselves to offshoring as they also have standardised procedures. These support services are not required to be close to the centre of banking activities and some parts are not essential, that is temporally simultaneous production, to conduct banking business.

The main reasons for captive offshoring are to reduce production costs while maintaining control over production, quality and proprietary information. This shifting of the cost base through the deployment of information and telecommunications technologies eliminates the spatial element and the temporal element may be overcome depending on the location of production in terms of time zone or whether the support service production is simultaneous with the banking services or may be delayed. The relative cost of telecommunications is much lower and combined with lower personnel expenses it is an attractive option for banks. Combined with the availability of qualified personnel and their relatively lower cost, and sometimes higher quality service, there is a strong motivating factor to offshore and, of course, it is a value adding factor for a bank. This type of foreign direct investment may also qualify for tax benefits or grants from the country of location.

The average compensation per employee in American non-bank service firms in the United States was $42,200 in 2000 and in foreign affiliates in developed countries $39,700 and in developing countries $25,000. This is an indication of the advantages, in terms of personnel expenses and the benefits to firms by producing abroad, between developing countries and other countries.[21]

There are other advantages in transferring intact an existing though a relatively expensive, in terms of costs, system of production as it continues the same support service production procedures and maintains the same interactions with other support services and the core banking divisions and reduces significantly costs of integration. The main costs of captive offshoring are mostly the initial cost of investment in premises and of training personnel. In the long run the reduction in the cost of production outweighs these. As only the largest banks may follow a strategy of captive offshoring, due to volume of output and the initial cost of relocating, they have a competitive advantage over other banks.

5

The Scope of International Bar Business Activities and Markets

International banking consists of the provision of banking services to non-residents and to residents in foreign currencies from offices located in the home country, as well as proprietary trading and on behalf of customers, without establishing a foreign presence. The types of services include domestic currency non-resident deposits and loans, foreign currency resident and non-resident deposits and loans, international payments and settlements, trade finance, foreign exchange, currency and bond trading and eurocurrency banking and correspondent banking.

A service provided by a bank located in one country to a customer located in another is considered a service export irrespective of the nationality of the bank or the customer or the currency of the transaction. The direction of the flow of the service export depends on the location of the customer. The criterion for measuring cross-border trade in banking services is the country of location of the bank where the service is produced and not the nationality of the bank. Indeed, nationality of a bank is difficult to define. It could be based on where the bank is incorporated, has its registered office, where the largest proportion of shareholders reside or when there is a holding company its location. The most practical definition of nationality of a bank is the location of the head office of the bank, or the bank holding company, as this is usually the country where the bank is incorporated and where it has its registered office, and where corporate policy is formulated and agreed.

Banks may be classified as international or multinational. A bank may be international, depending on type of banking service, the residency of the customer and the currency of the transaction, without being multinational. A multinational bank by definition is one with offices in more than one country. There are different levels of multinational banking hough. A bank that has foreign offices in a few countries that are in close geographic proximity, and which may also be close linguistically or culturally, or may have similar banking systems, and whose market reach and product reach is extensive in its home country and whose product reach may or may not be extensive in its foreign locations, is considered a regional multinational bank, and though it may have established an office in another continent, the majority of its business is in its home continent. Jurisdiction in the European Union refers to a single member state, that is where the bank is regulated. With a single financial market in the European Union, banks that have offices only in their own and in other member states are considered as European regional banks.

A global multinational bank is considered as one whose market reach and product reach is extensive in its home country and in its foreign locations, has offices in at least three continents and in the principal financial centres. Many banks have offices in offshore financial centres, sometimes only for booking purposes, and by definition these may be termed multinational, and often these shell branches or booking offices are merely departments of banks' international divisions. There is no interaction with local banking markets in which the office is located. Such booking offices alone do not constitute being classified as a multinational bank.

Ethnic banking, that is providing services to expatriates as the target market through foreign offices, is not considered multinational banking as it is specifically focusing on a minority of the potential foreign market and the range of services provided may be limited.

Eurobanks do not require a physical presence to conduct business. This type of business is offshore business and banks may establish offices in centres other than the leading international financial centres to access the markets at a lower cost. It is considered supranational international banking when the business being conducted is trading or intermediation, such as, in the eurocurrency money market, and supranational multinational banking when banks, primarily investment banks or universal banks, have a presence in the leading financial centres for originating, managing and participating in the eurobond market, an offshore capital market.

International and foreign claims

The Bank for International Settlements defines international claims as cross-border claims on residents outside the country of the office booking the claim and local claims in non-local currencies booked in banks' foreign offices. Foreign claims include these categories plus local claims in local currencies booked in foreign offices. Claims are on-balance sheet financial assets including loans and advances to banks and non-banks, and holdings of debt securities. They do not include derivatives. The various types are outlined in Figure 5.1.

In terms of securities markets the standard classification for bonds has been based on the location of the transaction, the currency of the issue and the residency or nationality of the issuer, that is bonds issued by resident issuers in domestic currency are classified as domestic bonds, by non-resident issuers in domestic currency as foreign bonds, and by resident and non-resident issuers in foreign currency as eurobonds. Of course, this is based on the residency of the issuer and not the investor. Allowing for the investor's residency the Bank for International Settlements has redefined these definitions for domestic currency issues and this is outlined in Figure 5.2.

Domestic and foreign bond issues that are aimed at non-resident investors are classified as eurobonds. This overcomes the difficulty of classifying a sterling bond issued by a resident British firm, listed in London and sold to non-residents. Though it is classified as a Eurobond to qualify as such trading must be over-the-counter only and

International Claims	Cross-border Claims on Residents outside the Country of the Bank Office Booking the Claim	Local Claims in non-Local Currencies in Foreign Offices

Foreign Claims	International Claims	Local Claims in Local Currency in Foreign Offices

Figure 5.1 International and Foreign Claims of Banks
Source: based on Bank for International Settlements, Consolidated Banking Statistics, Second Quarter 2004, p. 6

Bonds Issued in Domestic Currency		
Resident Issuer to Resident Investor	**Non-Resident Issuer to Resident Investor**	**Resident or Non-Resident Issuer to Non-Resident Investor**
Domestic	Foreign	Euro

Figure 5.2 Classification of Domestic, Foreign and Euro Bonds
Source: based on Bank for International Settlements, International Banking and Financial Market Developments, February 1997, p. 22

Domestic	Foreign	Euro
Issued Direct, by Auction or Syndicate	Domestic Syndicate	International Syndicate
Listed on Local Exchange	Listed on Local Exchange	Listed outside Local Exchange
Registered	Bearer Form or Registered	Bearer Form
Traded on Local Exchange*	Traded Over-the-Counter or on Local Exchange	Traded Over-the-Counter
Settlement through Local Clearing	Settlement through Local Clearing	Settlement through International Clearing

Figure 5.3 Features of Domestic, Foreign and Euro Bonds
* Government Paper may also be traded over-the-counter
Source: compiled from Bank for International Settlements, International Banking and Financial Market Developments, February 1997, p. 23

settlement must be outside the British financial system. The main features of each type of bond are outlined in Figure 5.3.

International and multinational banking

International trade in services for the balance of payments purposes is defined as between residents and non-residents and the Manual on Statistics of International Trade in Services extends this to include the value of services provided through foreign affiliates established abroad, which is termed foreign affiliates trade in services or FATS. Services are defined as heterogeneous products that do not have ownership rights, are produced to order, cannot be traded separately from their production and when they have been completley produced must have been supplied to the consumer. Some services though such as, advisory services and the storage and supply of information have ownership rights. Direct investment occurs when an investor in one country is the beneficial owner through ordinary shares or voting rights of more than 10% of a firm in another country. A subsidiary is a direct investment in a firm that is more than 50% owned. Branches are also included as direct investment.[1]

Most banks have foreign assets and liabilities, and therefore may be considered international. There are three categories of international banking according to Aliber.[2] One is based on location of business such that banks conduct domestic banking whenever they interact with customers in their country of origin regardless of the currency and conduct international banking when they transact business in foreign countries through foreign offices. Another is centred on the currency of the transaction. Domestic banking occurs when the currency of the transaction is the same nationality as that of the bank no matter where the transaction is conducted either in the home country or through a foreign office of the bank. The same bank, irrespective of location, is conducting international banking when the transaction is in a foreign currency. The third view differentiates the nationality of the customer and the bank. When they are the same the transaction is domestic, irrespective of the location of the transaction or the currency. When they differ the transaction is international. Aliber opts for the second concept of international, that is, when banks conduct business in currencies other than the currency of the nationality of the bank. The views are based on an industrial organisation approach focusing on foreign direct investment, and an intermediation approach focusing on cross-border and cross-currency flows.

Banks' foreign subsidiaries could be involved in pure domestic banking business in a foreign country according to Casson's typology of international banking as outlined in Figure 5.4. The fundamental features of international banking are based on differences between domestic and export banking, and determined by location of bank, residence of customer and currency of transaction.[3]

Country of Location of Bank and		
Residence of Customer	**Nationality of Currency**	**Type of International Banking**
Different	Different	Foreign Currency Export Banking
Different	Same	Home Currency Export Banking
Same	Different	Foreign Currency Domestic Banking

Figure 5.4 Typology of International Banking
Source: based on Casson, M., The Economic Theory of Multinational Banking, an Internalisation Approach, University of Reading, Department of Economics, Discussion Paper in International Investment and Business Studies, Volume II, Number 133, 1989, Table 1, p. 4

Banks conduct international, or export, banking when the residency of the customer, irrespective of the currency of the transaction, is different to the country of location of the bank. A variation of domestic banking occurs when the nationality of the currency of the transaction differs from country of location of the bank providing the service. There is no distinction between international and multinational banking.

This typology corresponds to that of Goodman. Domestic banking is the same for both; foreign currency domestic banking is equivalent to Goodman's definition of eurocurrency banking, home currency export banking equates to external banking, and foreign currency export banking is similar to eurocurrency and external banking. An exception to this category, which Goodman terms as offshore domestic banking, is when the nationality of the currency of the transaction is the same as the residency of the customer but the residency is different from the country of location of the bank providing the service.[4]

International banking is also classified by Lewis and Davis using the same criteria of nationality of currency, country of location of bank, residency of customer but additionally nationality of bank and type of banking, retail or wholesale. They categorise international banking as transactions with residents in foreign currencies and with non-residents in a domestic currency and consider eurobanking as comprising domestic and foreign banks located in a country transacting with residents and non-residents in that country in a currency other than the currency of the location of the bank.[5]

Euromarkets may be considered as a special category of multinational bank as the market is outside a bank's home market and banks could conduct business with non-residents in third currencies.[6] In contrast Jones considers eurobanking a form of international banking as the nationality of the bank, the currency and the customer may all differ and this corresponds to international banking.[7]

International services by tradability of output and ownership of production factors are the basis for categorising international banking by Ruane. Domestic banking consists of services produced by domestic factors and sold on domestic markets. Output produced by domestic factors and traded is considered trade in international banking services. Other services are produced using both domestic and foreign production factors and some of these are traded and others not. A service produced by both domestic and foreign factors and consumed in the country of production, that is not traded, is considered foreign direct investment and when it is traded it is considered both international trade and foreign direct investment. Most international banking services are in the category of domestic and foreign factors producing a non-traded output, with some others in both the domestic and foreign produced traded category and in the domestic produced and traded category. [8]

Factor movement is optional only when there are no, or low, barriers to trade or establishment or restrictions on foreign personnel. Managerial and technical knowledge, information, networks and resources and competencies are what are being traded according to Neu.[9]

There are three functions of multinational banks according to Grubel. These are multinational retail banking, multinational service banking and multinational wholesale banking. Multinational retail banking requires a network of foreign offices competing with local banks in domestic markets. The reasons for banks applying this strategy are due to advantages in management, technology, marketing know-how, and differentiated services. There are two motives for banks following a strategy of multinational service banking. One is based on banks following customers abroad for defensive purposes and internalising customer information and the other is to exploit information and provide services to foreign customers in the local banking market. The motivation for banks involvement in multinational wholesale banking is due to imperfections in international capital markets with opportunities for trading and arbitrage. This is closely associated with the euromarkets. Multinational banking is defined as the ownership of bank offices in a foreign country by a foreign bank.[10]

A report by the United Centre for Transnational Corporations, in 1988, defines a multinational bank, based on the criteria of type of office and geographic reach, as one with branches or majority owned subsidiaries in five or more foreign locations.[11] The definition of multinational banking by Gray and Gray is similar, though narrower. A bank is considered as multinational when it produces deposit and loan services in offices that are located in more than one country. This is also similar to Casson's definition which is the ownership and control of a bank in more than one country. The criterion of producing banking services in more than one country is also used in Jones' definition and restricts the type of office to a branch or a subsidiary.[12]

These definitions vary in criteria and scope in defining trade and foreign direct investment in banking. International trade in banking services may consist of cross-border trade, foreign direct investment, that is, multinational banking, or portfolio investment, such as, the purchase of foreign financial assets for the bank's own account or the acquisition of a minority shareholding in a foreign firm, bank or otherwise, without majority control.

While the number of offices, or the number of countries in which the bank has offices, are criteria used for defining a multinational bank it is market reach and product reach that are more relevant. This means that the type of office is also a determining factor. Multinational commercial banks usually have networks of branches or subsidiaries. Multinational investment banks have fewer offices, and these are regional centres through which they provide services in many countries to geographically disperse customers through the movement and temporary re-location of personnel to where the business is being conducted. The location of such offices is another factor, as it is important to be in different time zones for trading, and also important that these types of offices are capable of transacting business with local and foreign customers. A typology of trade in banking services and foreign direct investment by banks is outlined in Figure 5.5.

International Banking Markets

Foreign Trade	**Foreign Investment**	
Cross-Border Trade	**Direct Investment**	**Portfolio Investment**
International Banking	Multinational Banking	
Without Foreign Offices	With Foreign Offices	
Banking Services to non-residents irrespective of currency and to residents in foreign currencies	Banking Services to residents and non-residents from Foreign Offices in Foreign and Domestic Markets	Proprietary Investments in Financial and non-Financial Assets
	International Financial Centres	Minority Shareholdings in Financial and Non-Financial Foreign Firms for Bank's Own Account 10% or less
	Offshore Financial Centres	

Supranational Banking Markets

International Banking	Multinational Banking
Without Foreign Offices	With Foreign Offices
Euromarkets	Euromarkets
Trading	Leading, Managing and Participating in Corporate, Government and non-Governmental Agencies' Banking Business
Intermediation	

Figure 5.5 Typology of Trade in Banking Services and Foreign Investment by Banks

Supranational markets are non-regulated in the sense that there are no central regulatory authorities. It is of course an ordered market with rules of engagement and practices developed, and subsequently enhanced, by the participants.

Types of banks

Commercial banks activities are primarily based on intermediation and payment and settlements services. Commercial banks are involved in both retail and wholesale business activities. Their customers may be classified into two broad groups, individual and corporate. Individuals are personal customers whether acting in a sole capacity or with other persons. Private and public limited firms, governments, non-governmental agencies, supranational agencies and public authorities are considered corporate customers.

Retail banking services are provided by commercial banks to both categories of customer through a branch network. These networks are usually more extensive in the country of origin than in foreign countries although some banks have established retail banking networks abroad, mostly by acquiring a foreign bank. They may also establish a branch network *de novo* although this is rarer and it is usually focused on some market niche, such as, ethnic banking services to an expatriate community or on specific banking products and the range of activities is usually much narrower than in local banks. Wholesale commercial banking is largely between banks and other financial firms, in what is termed the inter-bank market. The inter-bank market is part of the money market where banks borrow and lend to each other to meet their respective funding requirements. Large non-financial firms and public authorities participate in the money markets by issuing short-term paper. The main features of the money market are that the instruments traded have short maturity and are highly liquid.

Notwithstanding their market reach, and while a large proportion of cross-border transactions by commercial banks is inter-bank, almost all commercial banks could be described as international as they conduct international payments and settlements on behalf of customers. A basic service such as foreign exchange is also international as it is transacting in a foreign currency in the domestic market. When customers transact business in another country with credit and debit cards, either when abroad or through the use of telecommunications, this may be termed personal international banking. Furthermore, most banks have an internet banking service and customers may transact banking services without being in the same country as the bank.

Investment banks operate principally in the capital markets and focus on corporate customers, such as, firms, institutional investors, governments and public authorities. Their main activities are underwriting and market making of securities issues, advising on capital raising and mergers and acquisitions, securities trading and institutional and investment fund asset management. Some investment banks also offer asset management services to high net worth individuals, which is often termed private banking when commercial banks provide this service. They are actively involved in wholesale banking markets.

Commercial and investment banks are intermediaries. Commercial banks make loans and investment banks underwrite and distribute securities issues. The relationship with their respective customers differs in that commercial banks hold loans as assets on their balance sheets, unless these are later securitised, whereas investment banks sell on issues they underwrite to investors in primary markets and also trade in securities in secondary markets.

In terms of revenue commercial banks, in general, obtain interest income and fee income and the type of services such as account and cash management may generate both types of income. Investment banks obtain revenue, as a fee, when it provides a service for a customer.

The relationship between the larger investment banks, the so-called 'bulge bracket' firms, is generally based on the size of the firm, the size of the transaction and the volume of transactions. The larger investment banks tend to provide services to larger firms due to the volume of activity although they also provide services to other firms when there is a transaction that requires their expertise because of the size or the complexity. So there are both relationships and unique transactions. There is also a prestige factor for customers to have a relationship with certain larger investment banks.

The nature of the relationship between an investment bank and customer is mostly a direct exchange of information between bank personnel and customer. This information is contained in personnel who could move to another bank so the nature of the long-term relationships is different.[14]

Unlike commercial banks investment banks do not have a deposits base to lend to customers. Instead it raises capital for its customers from investors. Investment banks compete and co-operate with each other. They compete for issuing business and then may co-operate in the distribution or selling of the issues through a syndicate of banks.

Commercial banks that conduct investment banking activities have significant advantages as their capital base is much larger. This was an issue that was to redefine investment banking in the 1980s and 1990s as many securities firms and investment banks went public thereby sourcing equity capital, whereas previously these firms had relied on partners' own capital. Prior to that, the New York stock exchange had prohibited member firms from being publicly owned. Investment banks also required increased capital to maintain their holding of securities and to compete internationally. By shifting to a permanent capital base they were also better placed to compete for the increasingly important institutional investors' business.[15]

Investment banks are managed through external networks of customers and competitor investment banks and internal networks of shared competencies and information. Of the 'free' services that investment banks provide, such as, research, a return is only realised when there is a transaction, what is termed a 'loose linkage'.[16]

A fully integrated universal bank provides a complete range of commercial and investment banking services and, especially in the German and Swiss models, has other additional aspects such as their cross shareholdings in non-financial firms and often a representative of the bank on the boards of firms. A universal bank, though, is a term that is used to describe a bank that comprises commercial and investment banking activities, whether it cross-shareholdings in non-financial firms or not. A bank may produce a limited range of both commercial and investment banking activities and, though nominally a universal bank, it is focusing on a narrow product market. Some commercial banks provide a limited range of investment banking services and though it is sometimes termed a universal bank its dominating business is commercial banking. It is not a fully integrated universal bank. Likewise investment banks may provide some commercial banking services and should not be considered as a fully integrated universal bank.

Universal banks and other banks that conduct a variety of either commercial banking activities, investment banking activities, securities business, insurance business or non-financial business are also termed conglomerates. A conglomerate financial services firm is one that consists of two or more types of financial firm, such as, a bank, a securities firm or an insurance firm and is regulated by different regulatory authorities. When a bank, whether a commercial bank or an investment bank, merges with or acquires an insurance firm it is considered a financial services conglomerate and the broad range of insurance services provided are comparable to the services provided for corporate and individual customers by other insurance firms. Allianz, the German insurance firm, acquired Dresdner Bank, a German universal bank, and is a leading international insurance firm and bank in its respective markets. *Allfinanz* is a term used usually to describe universal banking. *Bancassurance* is a similar term but is applied to a bank that also provides insurance services. When this insurance business is established *de novo* by a bank it is usually focused on general insurance and as such the *bancassureur* only competes with other insurance firms in a narrow range of products usually aimed at individuals. This insurance business would not constitute it being termed a conglomerate. Citigroup following the merger with Travelers, ING which also provides corporate and individual banking and insurance services, as well as, Allianz following the acquisition of Dresdner Bank are conglomerates. Similarly insurance firms, and indeed other non-financial firms, have established their own banks to provide a narrow range of commoditised retail banking services aimed at individuals.

The annex to the General Agreement on Trade in Services and the Second Banking Coordination Directive outline the main services that banks may provide. Both annexes are similar in the scope of services permitted. These services are accepting deposits and making loans, payment and money transmission services, guarantees and commitments, trading for own account or for account of customers in money market products, foreign exchange and derivatives, underwriting and placement of securities, advisory services, asset management, money broking, leasing and settlement and clearing services. These services are broadly in line with the services that commercial and investment banks provide as classified in Figure 5.6. That is, the principal services provided by commercial and investment banks are included in the agreements.

Parallel banks are banks that are not part of a financial group for consolidated regulatory purposes and are licensed in different jurisdictions, but have the same owner and often have closely linked business activities. They are established for tax purposes and sometimes to overcome legal restrictions associated with the establishment of foreign offices in some countries.

A non-financial firm may have a financial or banking subsidiary that is established for a specific type of business in niche markets. The most common types are established by retailers, whether they are heavy industry or technology retailers or large retail stores, for credit, consumer finance and for leasing purposes. Many of these issue their own commercial paper to fund these activities.

Corporate banks are established by non-financial firms to facilitate inter-company netting of accounts and clearing payments and settlements between subsidiaries, managing the firm's foreign exchange exposure and also its balance sheet, such as the issuing of commercial paper, and are also responsible for corporate financial risk management. They operate in wholesale banking markets.[13]

The determinants for the internationalisation of banking are based on country characteristics and market dynamics and bank-specific advantages. Primarily the country characteristics consist of barriers to entry to provide services, the type of activities allowed and the type of investment allowed, as well as, regulations on capital flows and taxation and repatriation of profits, or indeed, tax benefits offered by a government to attract foreign banks to invest directly to encourage spill-over effects in the industry. The size of the banking market and specifically the product markets that are targeted and the potential growth of these are other factors. In terms of the foreign financial market dynamics, the potential performance and profitability depends on the interaction and rivalry among existing banks in the market, the number of these, their nationality and their

International Commercial Banking

Principal Customers and Activities
Individual and Corporate Customers

Foreign Deposits and Lending including Syndicated Lending

Payments and Settlements

Trade Finance

Trading including for Own Account
- Money Markets
- Currencies
- Euromarkets
- Derivatives

Private Banking

International Investment Banking

Principal Customers and Activities
Corporate Customers

Capital Raising
Originating, Underwriting and Distributing Debt and Equity Securities

Market Making in Debt and Equity Securities

Trading including for Own Account
- Debt and Equity Securities
- Euromarkets
- Derivatives
- Currencies

Corporate Finance Advice
- Mergers and Acquisitions
- Initial Public Offerings and Debt and Equity Issuing

Institutional Asset Management and Own Fund Management

Figure 5.6 Typology of International Banks' Principal Customers and Banking Activities

Country Characteristics

Openness of Banking Market
Entry and Exit Barriers
Size of Banking Market and Potential Market Growth
Level of Development of Banking Market
Regulations on Bank Activities, Ownership and Capital Flows and Taxation
Location of International Financial Centre
Country Risk
Banking Stability
Exchange Rate Volatility
Trade Linkages

Banking Market Dynamics

Rivalry among Established Financial Firms
Pricing and Cost of Funds
Profitability of Product Type or Customer Type Market
Availability and Access to Substitute Suppliers and Products
Switching Costs for Customers
Foreign Direct Investment by other Financial Firms
Innovation

Bank Advantages

Brand and Reputation and Quality of Services
Access to Resources
Superior Capabilities and Management and Distinctive Competencies
Innovation in Products and Processes
Customer Focus

Figure 5.7 Country Characteristics, Banking Market Dynamics and Bank Advantages Affecting Bank Internationalisation

size distribution, that is, whether it is a concentrated oligopolistic market with a few large banks and some other smaller banks, or it is a highly fragmented market. Different product markets and customer segments, that is, individual or corporate customers, may have different levels of rivalry and margins and hence profitability is different for each type. The more a bank has distinctive competencies the more that they may be transferred abroad. By definition when the bank has distinctive competencies there must be some competitive advantage for the bank. Factors affecting bank internationalisation are outlined in Figure 5.7.

Organisation type of foreign bank offices

The most basic form of international trade in banking services is correspondent banking. This is essentially a foreign bank representing another bank in specific types of business and locations. Most banks have correspondent relations with foreign banks, and these are most often reciprocal relationships, in order to represent them in locations where they do not have offices. They hold deposits with each other in their respective local currencies. There is no requirement on the part of pure international banks to have a physical presence in any foreign location and many banks operate as international banks entirely through correspondent relationships. The main function of a correspondent bank is to provide collection and payment services which are often linked to international trade finance by their respective customers. They also refer business to each other as well as exchanging information on business opportunities in their respective countries and acting as liaison to match their respective customers in these business opportunities.

When banks decide to invest directly in a specific foreign location the form of the foreign office depends on strategy in terms of size of the investment and scope of services it intends to offer. The main types of foreign office are a representative office, an agency, a shell branch, a branch, a subsidiary or an affiliate or joint venture. Banks may follow a stage approach to their foreign direct investments, initially establishing *de novo* a representative office, then a branch and eventually a subsidiary, or establish *de novo* a subsidiary or merge with or acquire a foreign bank, depending on legal restrictions and its strategy in the foreign country.

The purpose of a bank's own representative office is to source new business and to gather information on foreign markets. This type of office does not actively engage in banking business. This is the initial step that banks make in establishing abroad.

An agency is an extension of a representative office and its business in almost entirely related to the financing of international trade. While an agency may lend, mostly inter-bank and to existing customers, such as, multinational firms, it may not accept deposits from local customers but may accept foreign deposits. This is the main difference between an agency and a representative office.

A branch is wholly owned, though not separately incorporated or capitalised, and may offer subject to local regulations a full range of banking services. Branches are licensed to provide a full range of banking services and regulated by the host country regulatory authority. The business of this type of structure tends to concentrate on trade finance, interbank lending and corporate lending. They are also a focal point for their large corporate customers when conducting business abroad. As well as being dependent on the parent bank for capitalisation, banking services are conducted in the name of the parent bank which has a legal obligation for all of its business.

A shell branch has no presence of management or administration in the country in which it is located and licensed, usually an offshore financial centre, and though some personnel may be assigned to it they are merely representatives for legal purposes. They are usually managed at a distance. They are typically not subject to supervision. A booking office is usually an administrative address for booking banking business to circumvent domestic restrictions on certain types of business. It is part of a bank that is regulated in its home country, although this may be circumvented by having the booking office managed by the bank through an office located in another country such that it is not regulated in its home country or where it is located and licensed. These types of offices do not interact with local banking markets.[17]

International Banking Facilities introduced in the United States in 1981 are in effect shell branches. The main business of this type of office is to allow American banks to conduct deposit and lending business in offshore dollars, specifically the Euromarkets, without being subject to reserve requirements or interest rate limits. They were introduced in an attempt to attract offshore business to the United States which was largely based in London in the Euromarkets and the dollar the main currency of such business. International Banking Facilities may be established by American banks and American branches and agencies of foreign banks. They may also be operated by Edge Act corporations.

Edge Act corporations were introduced in 1919 to facilitate interstate banking by a parent bank in international banking services thereby circumventing interstate banking regulations and also allowing banks to book business in lower tax states. This type of corporation is a subsidiary. American and foreign banks may establish such corporations. Like subsidiaries their banking activities are constrained by their own availability of capital and not that of the parent bank.

A subsidiary is a separate legal entity in which a bank has a controlling interest either through its shareholding or voting rights. Subsidiaries may offer a full range of banking services. Banks may establish foreign subsidiaries *de novo* or acquire an existing foreign bank. An acquired bank may continue to operate under its existing title or the acquiring bank may incorporate its title depending on the advantages to the bank. Citigroup has a wholly owned subsidiary in Mexico,

Banamex, and HSBC continued to operate as CCF in France having acquired it in 2000 although it is re-branding it as HSBC in 2005. Similarly, the Royal Bank of Scotland acquired National Westminster Bank and both banks operate under their own styles, Royal Bank of Scotland in Scotland and National Westminster Bank in the other regions of Great Britain.

Figure 5.8 outlines the various advantages of alternative forms of foreign direct investment. Branches and subsidiaries require substantial investment but offer greater control and these types of foreign office may offer a wider range of services.

A foreign affiliate bank is one in which a foreign bank holds a minority interest that is less than 50% of the controlling interest. When this type of foreign investment is less than 10% it is termed portfolio investment. The cross-shareholding that the Royal Bank of Scotland and BSCH of Spain had in their respective banks was portfolio investment. BSCH had to sell its share due to its bid for another British bank, Abbey, which it later acquired. The foreign bank affiliate of the investing bank is subject to regulation in the country in which it is located. The advantage of an affiliate is that it benefits from the expertise and contacts of its investing bank while maintaining information of local markets. This of course holds true for acquisitions of foreign banks when the acquired bank continues to operate in much the same manner as before the acquisition.

It is evident that a branch is the most favoured type of foreign direct investment among foreign banks from the larger member states of the European Union, and from the United States, Canada

	Representative Office	**Shell Branch**	**Branch**	**Subsidiary**	**Affiliate**
Amount of Investment Required	Modest	Minor/ Modest	Moderate/ Substantial	Moderate/ Substantial	Moderate
Control over Operation	Direct	Direct	Direct	Substantial/ Direct	Minor
Referral Business and New Business	Favourable	None	Favourable	Favourable	Minor/ Limited Potential

Figure 5.8 Relative Advantage of Alternative Foreign Offices
Source: based on Pecchioli, R., The Internationalisation of Banking, Organisation for Economic Cooperation and Development, Paris, 1983, Table 5, p. 61

Table 5.1 Favoured Type of Office* of Foreign Banks in London 2004 and New York 2003

		Type of Office – London			
Origin of Bank	**Number of Banks**	**Subsidiary**	**Branch**	**United Kingdom Incorporated**	**Representative Office**
European Union and Switzerland	101	5	69	13	14
United States and Canada	21	1	11	8	1
Japan	18	4	7	3	4
		Type of Office – New York			
	Total Number of Foreign Banks	**Subsidiary**	**Branch**	**Agency**	**Representative Office**
	218	22	114	23	59

* Some banks have more than one type of office and only the type considered the most important in terms of investment, resources and business activities is included.
Source: Compiled from The Banker, Foreign Banks in New York, May, 2003, and Foreign Banks in London, November, 2004

and Japan which have invested directly in London. In New York the most favoured type of office of foreign banks is a branch. Table 5.1outlines the distribution of the various types of offices of foreign banks in London and New York.

Organisation structure and business description of multinational banks

Most banks distinguish between individual, or personal, commercial and corporate customers in their organisation structure, as well as distinguishing corporate customers between small and medium sized firms and large firms, government, supranational and public authorities. However, the manner in which they organise themselves is quite different. A bank organises itself in a structure that complements its strategy and is considered the most efficient in terms of managing its business and financial reporting and delivering its services.

Selected international banks' businesses and organisation are outlined to illustrate the various forms through which international banks may organise themselves and the focus of their business internationally. These banks are representative of universal banks, commercial banks with limited investment banking activities, investment banks and conglomerate banks, and provide an insight into the differences, and also the similarities, in the management of their respective customers groups and the organisation of their respective banks. They are also selected on the basis of their nationality, that is, the location of their respective head offices, so that banks from Europe, the United States and Japan are represented. The banks selected are HSBC Holdings, a universal bank with its head offices in the United Kingdom, Barclays Bank, another British universal bank with origins in commercial banking and which, following the dissolution of BZW, Barclays de Zoete Wedd, its investment banking division comprising of its acquisition of de Zoete Wedd, a leading broker, prior to deregulation in the 1980s, has limited investment banking services concentrating on specific services, Deutsche Bank, a German universal bank, United Bank of Switzerland, a Swiss universal bank, Citigroup, a conglomerate bank with its head office in the United States, JPMorgan Chase, another American bank established though the merger of J.P. Morgan and Chase Bank, Goldman Sachs, an American investment bank, and the Japanese bank Mizuho Bank, which was established in 2000 following the merger of several banks. These banks are representative of commercial, investment and universal banking and of different regions and meet the criteria to be considered multinational banks.

HSBC Holdings[18]

Hongkong and Shanghai Banking Corporation was established in 1865 and expanded abroad mainly through acquisitions. It transferred its head office, HSBC Holdings, from Hong Kong to London in 1993 soon after acquiring Midland Bank. It has 9,500 offices in 79 countries and territories and is established in Europe, North America, Latin America, Africa, the Middle East, and of course in Asia Pacific, including Hong Kong.

The organisation structure is based on geographical regions and customer groups. There are five regions whose assets are distributed as follows: Europe 41.6%, North America, including Mexico, 28.3%, Hong Kong 19.3%, rest of Asia Pacific 9.6% and other Latin America 1.2%. Services are offered to four main customer groups, Personal Financial Services,

Commercial Banking, Corporate, Investment Banking and Markets, and Private Banking in these regions.

The principal operating companies of HSBC Holdings are HSBC Bank plc, which is principally focused on Europe and operates through the acquisitions of Midland Bank and CCF of France, HSBC North America Holdings, which is principally HSBC Bank USA, HSBC Bank Canada, HSBC Finance Corporation, and Grupo Financiero HSBC which is based on its Mexican operations and which is considered part of the North America region, HSBC Finance Netherlands, which is the reporting division for the operations of the HongKong and Shanghai Banking Corporation, Hang Seng Bank in Hong Kong, HSBC Bank Australia and the Middle East acquisitions, HSBC Investment Bank Holdings, HSBC Insurance Holdings, and HSBC Latin America Holdings which are the Brazilian and Argentinean businesses.

Customer group lines consist of Personal Financial Services accounts for 34.5% of assets, Commercial Banking which focuses on small and medium sized business including partnerships, associations and publicly quoted companies and accounts for 12.5% of assets, Corporate, Investment Banking and Markets, a division aimed at long-term relationships with corporate, supranational, government and institutional customers on a global scale and which accounts for 45.2% of assets, and Private Banking, a service for high net worth individuals accounting for 5.3% of assets, while other assets, the banks' own trust fund, accounts for 2.5%. The recent acquisition of Household International in North America now styled HSBC Finance Corporation is part of Personal Financial Services Group. HSBC's businesses usually operate as domestic banks with large retail deposit bases.

Personal Financial Services

Current accounts, deposit accounts and loans, payments, investment services, insurance consumer finance and credit and debit cards.

Commercial Banking Services

Payments and cash management, e-banking, wealth management, insurance, trade finance, leasing, invoice finance and factoring.

Corporate, Investment Banking and Markets Services

Lending including structured finance, 'large ticket' leasing, deposit services, treasury and capital market services, including foreign exchange, derivatives, money market instruments, equity trading and research, capital raising, investment banking services including corporate finance and advisory services and project and export finance, global transaction banking including payments and cash management services, securities services and global custody, and asset management services.

Private Banking Services

General banking services, investment services, global wealth services including financial and fiduciary planning and advice.

Barclays Bank[19]

Barclays Bank has a worldwide focus with 2,516 branches and is organised for reporting purposes in Strategic Business Units. These are supported by shared services. There are seven business groups or clusters and these are Personal Financial Services, Barclays Private Clients, Barclaycard, the credit card group, Business Banking, Barclays Africa, Barclays Capital, established following the divestment of BZW, and Barclays Global Investors.

Personal Financial Services Group

This is the retail banking division of Barclays in the United Kingdom and it has 14 million customers and provides a broad range of personal banking services.

Barclays Private Clients Group

This group focuses on high net worth individuals mostly in the United Kingdom and the rest of Europe. It provides personal banking services and asset management services to 1,060,000 customers. There have been some recent significant developments within this group through the establishment of First Caribbean in 2002, and the acquisition of the retail stockbroker Charles Schwab Europe in 2003 and also in 2003 the acquisition of the Spanish bank, Banco Zaragozano, to add to the existing Barclays Spain.

Barclaycard Group

Barclaycard, the bank's credit card business, operates in the United Kingdom and in the larger economies in Europe, such as France, Germany, Italy and Spain, and also in Africa, and provides services to individual and corporate customers, as well as, payment services to businesses. It has 11.4 million customers and 20% of credit cards issued in the United Kingdom are Barclaycards. Barclaycard International has issued 1.42 million credit cards.

Business Banking Group

This group focuses on providing banking services to large, medium and small firms in the United Kingdom, although services are also provided to these firms through business centres throughout Europe. There are 730,000 business customers representing a 21% market share.

Barclays Africa Group

Barclays Bank has offices in former British colonies in North Africa, sub-Saharan Africa and in countries in the Indian Ocean, and has recently transferred this region's head office from the United Kingdom to South Africa. It is an important international bank in this region with 1.5 million customers.

Barclays Bank strong in Africa through its long-term presence there, and through Barclays DCO, withdrew from its business in South Africa in the mid 1980s. It has re-entered this market through a strategic alliance between Barclaycard International and Standard Bank of South Africa and an acquisition of 60% of Absa, Amalgamated Banks of South Africa.

Barclays Capital Group

This group is the investment banking business of Barclays Banks and provides services to corporate, institutional and government customers. The business activities are divided into Rates, which provides services such as fixed income, foreign exchange, commodities, trading and research and equity related business, and Credit, which focuses on origination, sales, trading and research for loans, debt capital, structured capital markets and private equity. Barclays Capital is ranked fourth in global all debt rankings and is the leading issuer of sterling denominated bonds.

Barclays Global Investors Group

This group is the asset management business of Barclays and has more than 2,500 institutional customers in 47 countries. It also provides services, such as, securities lending and asset management. This group has more than $1 trillion in assets under management and contributed 60% of management fees and 50% of total income. It is the largest global institutional asset manager of assets held in hedge funds.

Deutsche Bank[20]

Deutsche Bank has essentially only two banking divisions and is organised as Corporate and Investment Bank and Private Clients and Asset

Management, as well as another division, Corporate Investments which is responsible for the bank's industrial shareholdings and other assets.

Corporate and Investment Bank

This division consists of Corporate Banking and Securities and Global Transaction Banking. Corporate Banking and Securities is the sub-division responsible for the corporate business of Global Markets, Global Equities, Global Corporate Finance and Global Banking. The services include capital markets, issuing, structured finance, lending and advisory business and the customers are private and public sector institutions as well as global firms and small and medium sized firms. The other sub-division is Global Transaction Banking includes such services as cash management, trade finance and trust and securities services.

Private Clients and Asset Management

This comprises two sub-divisions Private and Business Clients and Asset and Wealth Management. The Private and Business Clients sub-division offers banking services to private clients and small businesses. Its principal business is in Germany, Italy and Spain.

The Asset and Wealth Management sub-division comprises Asset Management, which provides services through the bank's global institutional asset management business and also through the retail businesses of DWS Investments in Europe and Scudder Investments in the United States, and Private Wealth Management which focuses on high net worth individuals.

United Bank of Switzerland[21]

United Bank of Switzerland was established following the merger of Union Bank of Switzerland and the Swiss Banking Corporation in 1999. There are four banking divisions and a corporate centre division. The four banking divisions are Wealth Management, Investment Bank, Global Asset Management and Wealth Management United States. The bank operates in five regions. In Switzerland, the location of the Corporate Centre, and in the rest of Europe and in Asia Pacific it provides services through the three divisons of Wealth Management, Investment Bank and Global Asset Management. In the United States its services are provided through these three banking divisions and also through the dedicated division Wealth Management United States. In Japan it provides investment banking services and global asset management services.

Wealth Management and Business Banking

In terms of the Wealth Management sub-division United Bank of Switzerland is the largest private bank in the world with 112 offices in Switzerland and 56 offices worldwide. The sub-division manages over $500 billion in invested assets. The Business Banking sub-division provides both retail and commercial banking services and is the leading bank in retail and commercial banking in Switzerland with 3.5 million individual account holders and also providing banking services to 180,000 businesses through 311 branches.

Investment Bank

The Investment Bank has headquarters in London and New York and is represented in 31 countries. There are three main business sub-divisions of the investment bank. These are Equities, Investment Banking, and Fixed Income, Rates and Currencies. The Equities sub-division is responsible for equity related business, including equity derivative products and equity research, in primary and secondary markets and is a member of more than 80 stock exchanges in the 31 countries in which the investment bank has offices. The Investment Banking sub-division is responsible for providing advisory services to worldwide corporate customers on mergers and acquisitions and corporate strategy. The Fixed Income, Rates and Currencies sub-division focuses on these type of services to firms and institutions in the regions in which United Bank of Switzerland is represented.

Global asset management

This division focuses on institutional and wholesale intermediary customers. This division is represented in 21 countries and the main offices are London, Chicago, New York, Tokyo and Zurich. This division's alternative and quantitative investment business includes hedge funds and its real estate business is responsible for property investment.

Wealth Management United States

The Wealth Management United States division has the fifth largest private client business in the United States and the almost two million customers are managed by 7,700 financial advisors located in 366 branch offices. The total amount in invested assets in this division is CHF 600 billion almost the same amount as the invested assets managed by the non-US Wealth Management sub-division in the rest of the world.

Citigroup[22]

In 1998 Citicorp merged with Travelers Group, an insurance firm, and formed Citigroup. It has offices in over 100 countries and in six continents. Globally the bank is organised into six regions and the income from each region is North America, 64%, Mexico, 8%, Europe, Middle East and Africa, 10%, Japan, 4%, Asia, 10%, Latin America 4%.

Citigroup is organised into five main business groups for internal financial reporting purposes with nine product lines offered within these. These are Global Consumer Services, including cards, consumer finance, retail banking and insurance, Global Corporate and Investment Bank, including capital markets and banking and transaction services, Private Client Services through Smith Barney, an acquisition, including services such as investment advice, financial planning and brokerage services to individuals, corporations and associations, and Global Investment Management, including insurance, private banking and asset management. The income from these business groups is distributed as follows: Global Consumer Services 55%, Global Corporate and Investment Bank 31%, Global Investment Management 10% and Private Client Services 4%.

The other internal financial reporting group, International, manages the group's product lines outside of North America and is organised into four geographic regions: Asia, Europe, Middle East and Africa, Japan and Latin America.

Global Consumer Services

The services provided are retail banking, consumer finance, commercial banking, leasing, credit and charge cards.

Global Corporate and Investment Bank Services

Capital Markets and Banking offers investment banking, underwriting and distributing equity, and debt and derivative securities debt and equity trading, institutional brokerage, advisory services, including acquisitions and mergers, foreign exchange derivatives and lending. Transaction banking comprises cash management, trade services, custody services and fund services to institutional investors, financial institutions, firms, and governments.

Private Client Services

This includes the provision of investment advice, financial planning and brokerage services to individuals and small, medium and large firms and not-for-profit organisations.

Global Investment Management

This business group offers insurance services and annuities through Travelers, the insurance firm with which Citicorp merged. The Private Bank provides services for high net worth customers including investment fund management, client trading, trust and fiduciary services, as well as a range of banking and lending services. Asset Management offers alternatives investment opportunities to high net worth customers and retail customers in such products as mutual funds investment trusts and hedge funds.

JPMorgan Chase[23]

JPMorgan Chase, has offices worldwide and is organised into five different business divisions. These are Investment Bank, Treasury and Securities Services, Investment Management and Private Banking, JPMorgan Partners and Chase Financial Services.

Investment Bank

The investment bank, JPMorgan, provides services for corporations, financial institutions, governments and institutional investors worldwide. The main services are advising firms, capital raising in equity and debt markets, market making in securities and derivatives and proprietary investing and trading.

Treasury and Securities Services

This business division comprises three sub-divisions. These are Trust Services, Investor Services and Treasury Services. Trust Services provides services, such as trustee and global securities clearance, to debt and equity issuers and to brokers and dealers. Investor Services provides services to mutual funds, plan funds, insurance firms and also to banks. The services comprise securities custody and securities lending. Treasury Services include such services as treasury management, cash management and liquidity management to corporations, financial institutions and governments.

Investment Management and Private Banking

This business is responsible for services to institutional investors, retail customers and high net worth individuals. There are two main subdivisions. These are JPMorgan Fleming Asset Management and JPMorgan Private Bank. JPMorgan Fleming Asset Management provides investment management services, online brokerage services and plan fund consultation and administration. JPMorgan Private Bank is responsible for providing services to private clients and these include wealth management, investment management, risk management, tax and estate planning and capital raising.

JPMorgan Partners

JPMorgan Partners is the bank's global private equity business, providing equity and mezzanine capital financing to private firms. It also invests in buyouts and ventures in all industries.

Chase Financial Services

This business focuses on personal customers and small and medium sized firms in the United States. It is a full service bank and also has consumer credit, mortgage, auto finance and card member subdivisions.

Goldman Sachs Group[24]

Goldman Sachs is one of the leading global investment banks, as well as being a securities and investment firm. It provides services to firms, financial institutions, governments and high net worth individuals. The firm is divided into three main businesses. These are Investment Banking, which provides a wide range of investment banking services, Trading and Principal Investments, and Asset Management and Securities Services. The Trading and Principal Investments business focuses on proprietary market making in and trading of fixed income and equity products, currencies and commodities, as well as being actively involved in derivatives. It is also a clearer for customer transactions on the leading stock, options and futures exchanges and is also a leading investor through the funds it manages. The Asset Management and Securities Services business provides advisory services as well as brokerage, financing and securities lending services to mutual funds, plan funds, hedge funds and to high net worth individuals.

Mizuho Financial Group[25]

The Mizuho Financial Group was established in 2000 through the merger of Dai Ichi Kangyo Bank, Fuji Bank and the Industrial Bank of Japan. There are three main business activity divisions in this financial group. These are the Banking and Securities Business Sector, the Trust and Asset Management Business Sector and Strategic Subsidiaries.

The bank is organised into Mizuho Corporate Bank, MHCB, and Mizuho Bank, MHBK, part of the Banking and Securities Business Sector, and there are also other units such as Mizuho Securities, also part of the same sector, and Mizuho Trust and Banking, part of the Trust and Asset Management Business Sector, as well as, other units in the Strategic Subsidiaries division, such as, the card and venture capital subsidiaries.

Mizuho Corporate Bank focuses on large Japanese firms and their foreign subsidiaries, foreign firms, financial institutions and public sector entities. Mizuho Bank provides service for individuals, Japanese firms and local governments.

Mizuho Corporate Bank

There are eight separate units in this division. These are Corporate Banking, International Banking, focusing on foreign firms and foreign subsidiaries of Japanese firms, Financial Institutions and Public Sector unit, Syndicated Finance Business unit, providing loan-related services in Japan and abroad, Financial Products unit, Asset Management and Transaction Banking unit, including e-business services, yen clearing and custody services and currency related services, along with the Asset and Liability Management and Trading unit and the Corporate Restructuring Business unit.

Mizuho Bank

There are eight separate groups in the Mizuho Bank division. These are the Customer and Private Banking group which focuses on individuals, the Corporate Banking group, which focuses on Japanese small and medium sized firms, the Public Sector Banking group, which provides services for local governments and national public sector entities, the Trading and Asset and Liability Management group, the Securities and Investment Banking group, focusing on corporate bond finance, trustee and administration business of corporate bonds, the Trust and Asset Management group, the Trade Services group, primarily focused on foreign exchange, foreign currency related business and trade finance, and the e-Business Services group.

Mizuho Securities

This is a wholesale securities firm whose customers are institutional investors, firms, financial institutions and public corporations. The business of this division is bond and stock trading, debt and equity financing, structured finance and advisory services.

Mizuho Trust and Banking

This is a trust bank and its principal business activities are private banking, asset management for individuals, custody and securitisation.

International banking and securities markets

In 1995 net international bank lending, among the Group of Ten countries plus 14 other countries including offshore banking centres, accounted for 62.5% of total international financing, with net international bond financing accounting for 30% and net euronote placements for 7.5%.[26]

In 2003 international banking assets of 28 reporting countries, including eight offshore centres, were 61% of total international banking and securities markets while securities markets accounted for 39%. This is outlined in Table 5.2.

The majority of external assets and local assets in foreign currency assets, 63%, were inter-bank. A higher proportion of liabilities, 71%, were inter-bank. The data for non-bank and inter-bank assets and liabilities are outlined in Table 5.3.

In terms of securities markets the amount of issues outstanding is dominated by financial institutions as issuers in developed countries. Of the total amounts of securities outstanding, 89% were issued by firms and governments in developed countries, with 71% issued by financial institutions. Tables 5.4 and 5.5 outline international securities markets by nationality of issuer and type of issue, respectively.

Commercial paper is by the far the dominant type of issue in money markets and straight fixed bonds dominate capital markets.

The data presented in Table 5.6 illustrates the wide variations in commercial banking profitability between countries and by different measures of profitability. Interestingly, these are quite pronounced between the six European Union Member States,

Table 5.2 International Banking and Securities Markets* 2003 Amounts Outstanding of Banks US Dollar Billions end year

	Amount	Percentage
Total International Banking and Securities Markets	29,940	
Banking Markets	18,268	61
Securities Markets	11,672	39
of which		
International Money Market Instruments	569	2
International Bonds and Notes	11,103	37

* The reporting countries include 20 developed countries and eight countries considered as offshore centres

Source: Bank for International Settlements, Quarterly Review, Statistical Annex, June 2004, Tables 1, 12A, 13A and 13B

Table 5.3 International Banking Market 2003
Amounts Outstanding of Banks US Dollar Billions End Year

Total International Positions – Assets						
External Loans and Deposits		**External Holdings of Securities and other**		**Local Assets in Foreign Currency**		**Total**
Non-Bank	Inter-bank	Non-Bank	Inter-bank	Non-Bank	Inter-bank	
3,035	8,767	2,638	1,489	1,035	1,304	18,268
External Assets and Local Assets in Foreign Currency						
Total Non-Bank			**Total Inter-Bank**			
6,708			11,566			
Total International Positions – Liabilities						
External Loans and Deposits		**Own Issues of Securities and other**		**Local Assets in Foreign Currency**		**Total**
Non-Bank	Inter-bank	Non-Bank	Inter-bank	Non-Bank	Inter-bank	
3,880	9,581	354	1,513	980	1,662	17,970
External Liabilities and Local Liabilities in Foreign Currency						
Total Non-Bank			**Total Inter-Bank**			
5,214			12,756			

Source: calculated from Bank for International Settlements, Quarterly Review, June 2004, Table 1

Table 5.4 International Securities Markets by Nationality of Issuer 2003
Amounts Outstanding US Dollar Billions End Year

Region	Total	of which Financial Institutions	of which Corporate Issuers	of which Governments
Total	11,672	8,538	1,495	1,131
Developed Countries	10,394	8,275	1,350	769
Developing Countries	638	173	123	342
Offshore Centres	133	90	22	20
International Organisations	507	–	–	–

Source: Bank for International Settlements, Quarterly Review, Statistical Annex, June 2004, Tables 12 A, 12 B, 12 C and 12 D

suggesting that a single banking market is far from complete and the segmentation of banking markets is based on country especially when comparing net interest margin. American banks are ranked highest in terms of pre-tax profits and net interest margin, although with the highest operating costs, and German and Japanese banks ranked lowest on pre-tax profits and also the lowest on net interest margin and operating costs.

Table 5.5 International Securities Markets by Type of Issue 2003 Amounts Outstanding US Dollar Billions and Percentage End Year

	Amounts Outstanding	Percentage of which Commercial Paper	Percentage of which Floating Rate	Percentage of which Straight Fixed Rate
Money market Instruments	569	73.5		
Bonds and Notes	11,103		25.7	71.1
Total	11,672			

Source: Bank for International Settlements, Quarterly Review, Statistical Annex, June 2004, Tables 13 A and 13 B

Table 5.6 Profitability of Commercial Banks 2003 Percentage of Total Average Assets Selected Countries

Country and Number of Banks	Pre-tax Profits	Net Interest Margin	Operating Costs
United States (11)	2.04	2.99	3.41
Spain (3)	1.27	2.38	2.12
United Kingdom (4)	1.22	1.82	2.12
Canada (5)	1.00	1.99	2.78
Italy (5)	0.81	2.05	2.52
Netherlands (3)	0.65	1.63	1.86
Switzerland (2)	0.63	0.88	2.03
France (3)	0.58	0.91	1.55
Japan (11)	0.07	0.55	0.80
Germany (4)	–0.20	0.79	1.66

Source: Bank for International Settlements, Annual Report, 2004, Table VII.1

Part IV

Competitive Advantage in International Banking

6
The Leading International Banks

Comparative advantage is associated with the theory of international trade and refers to the advantages that countries have in the production of particular products and does not focus on firms. Countries do not compete in international business, although there is tax competition. It is firms from particular countries that compete and have competitive advantages. One of the ways in which banks compete is through service quality.

International banking market and product reach

Competition in international banking is based on market reach and product reach and quality. In any national market the interaction of the various strategic groups could be as illustrated in Figure 6.1. Indigenous, including foreign owned indigenous banks, and foreign banks are in specific groups with some overlap depending on the breadth and depth of services provided from universal banks offering commercial and investment banking services to commercial banks, independent investment banks, to commercial banks offering some investment banking services and foreign banks in niche commercial or niche investment banking markets. The depth and breadth of services could vary, of course, and these could vary between countries depending on the individual bank strategies and the national regulations.

International investment banking is often conducted through the temporary presence of bank personnel in a foreign country for a specific purpose without establishing a foreign office in that country. A foreign investment bank may act solely as advisors to a government, a public authority or a firm, thereby competing with indigenous investment banks based on some distinctive advantage. There may not be direct

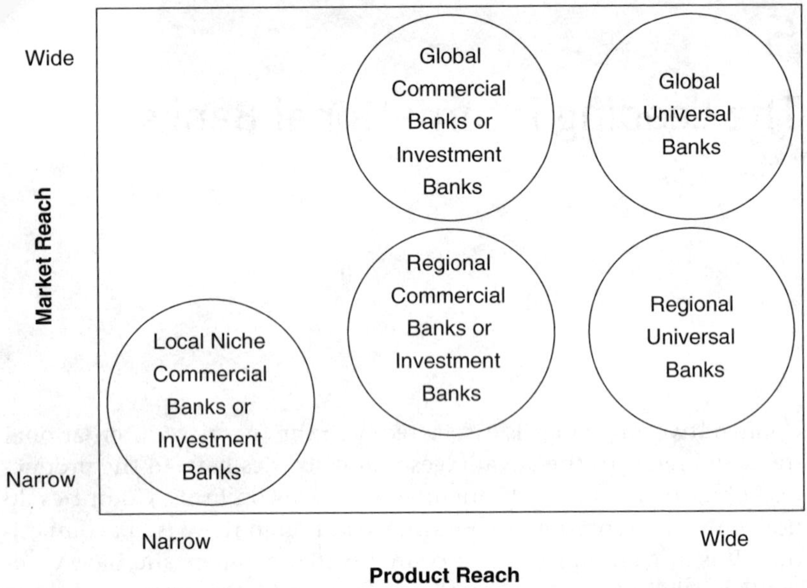

Figure 6.1 Market and Product Reach of Banks

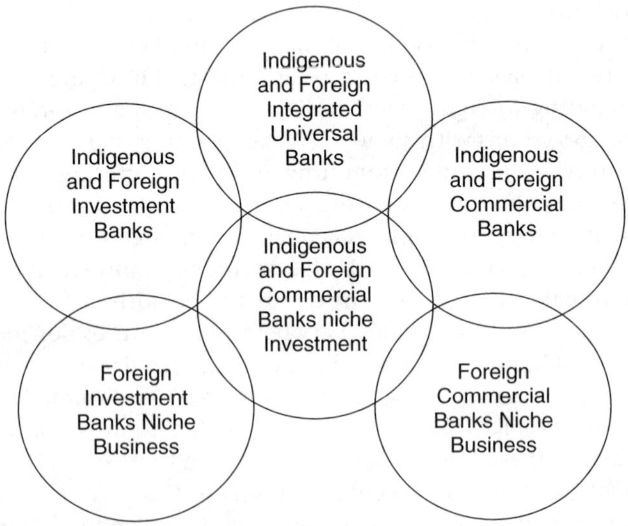

Figure 6.2 Strategic Groups of Banks Competing in National Banking Markets

competition, of course, as indigenous investment banks may be restricted by size or they may not have the competencies to provide specific services. Alternatively, indigenous investment banks may seek partner foreign investment banks so that it may provide a specific service thereby temporarily importing the competencies.

Being in a different strategic group does not necessarily mean that strategic groups of banks are not in competition with each other. Commercial banks that provide limited investment bank services and universal banks that provide commercial and investment bank services, whether in national or foreign markets compete. A global universal bank with commercial banking activities in a foreign market is in competition with local commercial banks. The possible overlap in national markets between different strategic product groups of banks is illustrated in Figure 6.2.

Competitive advantage in services among international banks

To determine competitiveness in international banking, and those banks considered to be the most competitive and the best, the leading 50 banks ranked by either asset size or Tier 1 capital are selected. These are the initial criteria for inclusion. The analysis of these banks also includes their rankings based on the proportion of their assets that are foreign.

The banks are then ranked based on their competitiveness, in terms of quality, in selected business activities. A broad range of commercial banking and investment banking business activities is included so that commercial banks, investment banks, universal banks and specialist private banks are represented. The services included are syndicated lending, capital raising, international bonds, advisory services, project finance, foreign exchange, private banking and global debt and equity.

Table 6.1 outlines the region of origin of the leading 1,000 banks in the world. This ranking is based on Tier 1 capital, or strength of the bank. More than a third of the banks originates from the European Union and Switzerland with almost a quarter from North America, that is, the United States and Canada. When Japan is included with these regions the total number of banks ranked among the leading 1,000 increases to more than two thirds. North American banks have increased their share from 18.2% in 1996 and banks from the European Union and Switzerland have declined in share from 42.2%. Japanese banks' share declined in share from 21%. These banks account for almost 69.6% of the total number of banks in 2004 which is a decline

Table 6.1 Proportion of Banks in the Leading 1000 World Banks by Origin 2004

Origin of Bank	Percentage of Banks
European Union 15 and Switzerland	34.6
United States and Canada	23.7
Japan	11.3
Total	69.6
Other Regions	30.4

Source: The Banker, Top 1000 World Banks, July 2004

from 1996 when they accounted for 81.4%. This is partly due to consolidation among banks in these countries.

The criteria of being among the leading 50 banks based on either asset size and Tier 1 capital is the basis for determining the banks that have the size and strength to compete among the leading banks in international banking. These are outlined in Table 6.2 and ranked by assets. These banks assets range from $1,285 billion to $189 billion. In total 56 banks meet these criteria.

The leading 50 banks ranked by size of assets are also ranked among the leading 50 banks based on Tier 1 capital except six banks, Abbey

Table 6.2 Banks Ranked in the Leading 50 by Assets or Tier 1 Capital 2004

Bank	Country of Origin	Rank by Assets
Mizuho Financial Group	Japan	1
Citigroup	United States	2
United Bank of Switzerland	Switzerland	3
Crédit Agricole	France	4
HSBC Holdings	United Kingdom	5
Deutsche Bank	Germany	6
BNP Paribas	France	7
Mitsubishi Tokyo Financial Group***	Japan	8
Sumitomo Mitsui Financial Group	Japan	9
Bank of America*	United States	10
Royal Bank of Scotland	United Kingdom	11
Barclays Bank	United Kingdom	12
Crédit Suisse	Switzerland	13
JPMorgan Chase	United States	14
UFJ Holdings***	Japan	15
ING Bank	Netherlands	16
Société Générale	France	17
ABN AMRO Bank	Netherlands	18

Table 6.2 Banks Ranked in the Leading 50 by Assets or Tier 1 Capital 2004 – *continued*

Bank	Country of Origin	Rank by Assets
HBOS	United Kingdom	19
Industrial and Commercial Bank of China	China	20
HypoVereinsbank	Germany	21
Dresdner Bank	Germany	22
Fortis Bank	Belgium	23
Rabobank	Netherlands	24
Commerzbank	Germany	25
Groupe Caisse d'Epargne	France	26
Norichunkin Bank	Japan	27
Bank of China	China	28
Lloyds TSB Group	United Kingdom	29
Crédit Mutuel	France	30
Banco Santander Central Hispano	Spain	31
Dexia	Belgium	32
China Construction Bank	China	33
Deutsche Zentral-Genossenschaftsbank	Germany	34
Landesbank Baden-Württemberg	Germany	35
Wachovia Corporaton	United States	36
Bayerische Landesbank	Germany	37
Wells Fargo	United States	38
Resona Holdings	Japan	39
BBVA	Spain	40
Agricltural Bank of China	China	41
Nordea Group	Sweden	42
Banca Intesa	Italy	43
Metlife	United States	44
Bank One Corporation**	United States	45
West LB	Germany	46
Abbey National	United Kingdom	47
Danske Bank	Denmark	48
UniCredito	Italy	49
Royal Bank of Canada	Canada	50
Banque Populaire	France	51
Washington Mutual	United States	54
National Australia Bank	Australia	55
SanPaolo IMI	Italy	57
Scotiabank	Canada	61
US Bancorp	United States	67

* Bank of America ranked 15 acquired FleetBoston ranked 64 in 2003 and have been consolidated
** Merged with JPMorgan Chase in 2004
*** Mitsubishi Tokyo Financial Group acquired UFJ Holdings in 2005
Source: The Banker, Top 1000 World Banks, July 2004

National ranked 53 on Tier 1 capital, Landesbank Baden-Württemberg ranked 54, Danske Bank ranked 55, Dresdner Bank 59, DZ Bank ranked 61, and Resona Holdings ranked 62. The banks that are ranked in the leading 50 banks based on Tier 1 capital but ranked outside the leading 50 banks based on assets are Banque Populaire, Washington Mutual, National Australia Bank, SanPaolo IMI, Scotiabank, and US Bancorp. The 56 banks represented in Table 6.2 are ranked by country of origin in Table 6.3 and region of origin in Table 6.4. There are 15 countries represented. Almost two thirds of these banks are clustered in five countries, the United States, Germany, Japan, the United Kingdom and France.

There is a wide variation in the amount of total assets of the largest bank between countries. The range of total assets in some countries is also quite narrow where the banks represented are of similar size. In the six countries where the largest bank has assets of $1,000 billion or more the range between banks is wide.

The proportional differential between the number of banks ranked in the leading 50 by either assets or Tier 1 capital and those ranked in the leading 1,000 is illustrated in Table 6.4. There is a wide variation in the proportion of banks from the European Union and Switzerland, almost

Table 6.3 Banks Ranked in Leading 50 by Assets or Tier 1 Capital and Range of Assets by Country of Origin 2004

Country of Origin	Number of Banks	Range of Total Assets Highest and Lowest Banks US Dollar Billions
United States	10	1,264–189
Germany	8	1,015–602
Japan	6	1,285–359
United Kingdom	6	1,034–315
France	5	1,105–300
China	4	638–360
Italy	3	329–256
Netherlands	3	684–509
Belgium	2	535–442
Canada	2	301–211
Spain	2	444–363
Switzerland	2	1,121–778
Australia	1	265
Denmark	1	307
Sweden	1	331
Total	56	

Source: The Banker, Top 1000 World Banks, July 2004

60%, compared to other regions. This narrows to a third when banks are ranked in the leading 1,000. A larger proportion, almost 10%, of banks from the European Union and Switzerland are ranked in the leading 50 than from North America, 5%, and Japan, 5.3%. In absolute terms there are almost three times as many banks from the European Union and Switzerland in the leading 50 than from North America. There are also almost as many banks from the European Union and Switzerland as North America and Japan together ranked in the leading 1,000 and almost twice the number ranked in the leading 50. The data suggest that there are more large banks in the European Union and Switzerland relative to the number of small and medium sized banks than in North America or Japan. The only countries represented in Tables 6.3 that are outside the European Union, Switzerland, the United States, Canada or Japan, are China with four banks and Australia with one bank.

Being ranked by asset size and Tier 1 capital does not mean that a bank is international in focus, although these banks should be located in the main international financial centres, have their own international networks and a large proportion of their assets abroad. The notable exceptions among these 56 banks are the four Chinese banks. In addition having a large asset base does not mean that these assets are foreign. It could also be that a bank has a large volume of foreign assets but that these are a relatively lower proportion of total assets, relative to other banks with a lower volume of foreign assets, due to the dominance of the bank in its domestic market and especially when this

Table 6.4 Banks Ranked in Leading 50 and 1000 Banks by Assets or Tier 1 Capital Ranked by Origin, Number and Proportion 2004

	Number of Banks	Leading 50 Banks by Assets or Tier One Capital Percentage	Number of Banks	Leading 1000 Percentage
European Union and Switzerland	33	58.9	346	34.6
United States and Canada	12	21.4	237	23.7
Japan	6	10.7	113	11.3
Other	5	9.0	304	30.4
Total	56		1,000	

Source: The Banker, Top 1000 World Banks, July 2004

is a large domestic market. For instance, Citigroup has only 34.2% of its assets as foreign assets although it is one of the most widely represented banks worldwide and in a wide range of financial markets. This relatively low proportion is due to its large domestic assets. Conversely, United Bank of Switzerland has 84.1% of its assets as foreign assets and also has a dominant position in its domestic market. The difference is that the size of its domestic financial market compared to the United States distorts the comparative proportions. However, the fact that their markets differ in size should not detract from the international focus of either of these banks. The proportion of foreign assets held by banks does count as a measure of a bank's international focus through committing to foreign markets and customers. There are only 17 banks among the leading 50 banks ranked by either assets or Tier 1 capital that have more than 30% of their assets as foreign assets. These are outlined in Table 6.5 with their rankings. These banks have a truly international focus.

Table 6.5 Banks Ranked by Proportion of Foreign Assets* and Total Assets 2004

Bank	Rank by Percentage of Foreign Assets	Rank by Total Assets
United Bank of Switzerland	1	3
Crédit Suisse	2	12
Deutsche Bank	3	6
ABN AMRO Bank**	4	18
BNP Paribas	5	7
HSBC Holdings***	6	5
ING Bank	7	16
BSCH	8	31
Scotiabank	9	61
National Australia Bank	10	55
Fortis Bank	11	23
BBVA***	12	40
Royal Bank of Canada	13	50
Dresdner Bank	14	22
Citigroup	15	2
Royal Bank of Scotland	16	10
Société Générale	17	17

* Only banks with a proportion of assets of more than 30% of their assets are ranked
** Average interest bearing assets
*** outside Europe
Source: The Banker, Top 1000 World Banks, July 2004, Top Global Banks, February 2003

Citigroup, one of the largest international banks, is only ranked 33rd among all banks in terms of the proportion of its assets abroad although it is ranked second in terms of the size of its total assets due to the large franchise it has in the United States. This is similar for the Royal Bank of Scotland and Société Générale, although another French bank, BNP Paribas is ranked relatively higher in terms of total assets and the proportion of its assets that are foreign. Only seven banks have more than 50% of their total assets abroad.

Having an international focus by having a large proportion of foreign assets differs from being an internationally competitive bank. To be considered as such banks must provide customers with a wide range of banking services including services considered to be representative of commercial banking, investment banking and private banking. Independent investment banks are effectively excluded from the rankings based on assets or Tier 1 capital.

A broad range of banking services is selected to determine the most competitive banks. This allows all types of banks to be represented. Table 6.6 outlines the banks ranked among the leading 10 banks by various types of business activity. Banks may be ranked in all or some of the ten business activities. There are 30 banks in total represented.

There are only 15 banks of the 30 banks represented ranked in three or more business activities. One of the 30 banks is an independent private bank and therefore is ranked in one business activity. This is the Swiss private bank, Pictet, and is ranked 7th in private banking and is the only independent private bank ranked in this category. The leading banks in terms of frequency of representation are outlined in Table 6.7. The total represents the leading 10 banks in each of the 10 business activity categories.

There are 15 banks from the European Union and Switzerland, 10 North American banks, three Japanese and two Australian banks among these 30 banks. The rankings are dominated though by a few banks. Of the 15 banks that are represented in three or more categories, eight are from the European Union and Switzerland, six from North America and one from Japan.

Those banks that have a proportion of 30% or more of assets as foreign assets or that are also ranked in three or more of the business activities are considered the leading competitive global banks.

There are 17 banks that have 30% or more of their assets as foreign assets. Of these only nine banks are also ranked in three or more business activities. There are nine banks whose proportion of foreign assets is more than 30% but are ranked in less than three business

Table 6.6 Leading Banks by Business Activity 2004

Bank	Assets	Percentage of Assets Foreign	Global Syndicated Loans	Capital Raising	International Bonds	Global Adviser	Global Project Finance	Foreign Exchange	Private Banking	Global Debt, Equity and Equity Related
ABN AMRO	–	4	–	7	–	–	–	–	10	–
Bank of America	–	–	3	–	–	–	–	–	–	10
Bank One	–	–	7	–	–	–	–	–	–	–
Barclays Bank	–	–	5	3	8	–	9	7	–	–
BNP Paribas	7	5	8	–	–	–	8	–	9	–
BSCH	–	8	–	–	–	–	–	–	–	–
Citigroup	2	–	2	1	1	3	2	3	2	1
Crédit Agricole	4	–	–	–	–	–	3	–	–	–
Crédit Suisse	–	2	–	10	6	9	–	8	4	6
Deutsche Bank	6	3	4	2	2	10	4	2	6	7
Dresdner	–	–	–	–	–	–	–	–	–	–
Goldman Sachs	–	–	–	6	–	1	–	6	8	9
HSBC	5	6	9	9	10	–	–	5	3	–
ING	–	7	–	–	–	–	–	–	–	–
JPMorgan Chase	–	–	1	4	4	4	–	4	5	4
Lazard	–	–	–	–	–	6	–	–	–	–
Lehman	–	–	–	–	7	8	–	–	–	5
Merrill Lynch	–	–	–	–	5	5	–	10	–	3
Mitsubishi Tokyo	8	–	–	–	–	–	–	–	–	–
Mizuho	1	–	6	–	–	–	–	–	–	–
Morgan Stanley	–	–	–	8	3	2	–	–	–	2
National Australia Bank	–	10	–	–	–	–	–	–	–	–
Pictet	–	–	–	–	–	–	–	–	7	–
Royal Bank of Scotland	10	–	–	–	–	–	1	9	–	–
Scotiabank	–	9	–	–	–	–	–	–	–	–
Société Générale	–	–	–	–	–	–	7	–	–	–
Sumitomo Mitsui	9	–	10	–	–	–	10	–	–	–
UBS	3	1	–	5	9	7	–	1	1	8
West LB	–	–	–	–	–	–	5	–	–	–
Westpac Banking	–	–	–	–	–	–	6	–	–	–

Global Syndicated Loans – ranking by proceeds, International Bonds – ranking by proceeds amount and overallotment sold in all currencies except US global, Global Adviser – ranking by value, Mandated Arrangers for Global Project Finance – ranking by loan amount, Global Debt, Equity and Equity Related – proceeds amount

Source: Total Assets, The Banker, July 2004, Foreign Assets, The Banker, July 2004, Foreign Exchange, Euromoney, May 2004, Capital Raising, Euromoney, October 2004, Private Banking: Best Private Banks Worldwide, Management Today, May 2004, Mandated Arrangers for Global Project Finance, Global Debt, Equity and Equity Related, Global Syndicated Loans, Global Adviser and International Bonds, The Finance Director's Guide to Global Banking 2004, Global Finance, 2004

Table 6.7 Frequency of Banks Ranked among the Best Banks by Business Activity 2004

Bank	Frequency
Deutsche Bank	10
Citigroup	9
UBS	8
Crédit Suisse	7
HSBC	7
JPMorgan Chase	7
Barclays Bank	5
BNP Paribas	5
Goldman Sachs*	5
Merrill Lynch*	4
Morgan Stanley*	4
Lehman*	3
Royal Bank of Scotland	3
Sumitomo Mitsui	3
ABN AMRO	3
Bank of America	2
Crédit Agricole	2
Mizuho	2
BSCH	1
Bank One	1
ING	1
Lazard	1
Mitsubishi Tokyo	1
National Australia Bank	1
Pictet	1
Scotiabank	1
Société Générale	1
West LB	1
Westpac Banking	1
Total	100

* Ranked in only eight business activities. Not ranked by assets or percentage of assets that are foreign

activity categories. Six other banks are ranked in three or more business activities but not by the proportion of foreign assets. These 24 banks are outlined in Table 6.8 and grouped by origin in Table 6.9 and are considered the leading banks in international banking. The 24 banks represent 11 different countries. There are six American banks, three British banks, two banks from Canada, France, Germany, the Netherlands, Spain and Switzerland, and one bank from Belgium, Australia and Japan.

Table 6.8 Banks Ranked by 30% or More of Foreign Assets and in Three or More Business Activities 2004

Banks Ranked by 30% or more Foreign Assets and Ranked in 3 or more Business Activities	Banks Ranked by 30% or more Foreign Assets only	Ranked in 3 or more Business Activities only
BNP Paribas		
Crédit Suisse		
Citigroup		
Deutsche Bank		
HSBC Holdings		
United Bank of Switzerland		
Royal Bank of Scotland		
ABN AMRO Bank		
BBVA		
	BSCH	
	Dresdner Bank	
	Fortis Bank	
	ING Bank	
	National Australia Bank	
	Royal Bank of Canada	
	Scotiabank	
	Société Générale	
	Barclays Bank	
		Goldman Sachs*
		JPMorgan Chase
		Lehman*
		Merrill Lynch*
		Morgan Stanley*
		Sumitomo Mitsui

* These investment banks are ranked in this category only.

Table 6.9 Leading 24 Banks in International Banking 2004

Origin	Number of Banks
European Union and Switzerland	14
North America	8
Japan	1
Australia	1

Although the criteria of the proportion of foreign assets and the ranking in selected business activities for inclusion in ascertaining the leading banks in international banking are limited, the ranking of banks based on these criteria allows a comparison of banks. The business activities are representative of services provided by international banks and the rankings of banks by these business activities are based on the opinions of their peers.

These leading banks provide a wide range of banking services through worldwide offices to a broad range of customers in geographically and temporally segmented markets. Many of these leading banks are the result of recent mergers and acquisitions as outlined in Table 6.10.

Table 6.10 Leading Banks through Recent Mergers and Acquisitions

Bank	Component Merged or Acquired Bank
ABN AMRO	ABN and AMRO merger and La Salle Bank acquisition
BBVA	Banco Bilbao Vizcaya and Argentaria merger and Bancomer acquisition
BNP-Paribas	Paribas acquisition
BSCH	Banco Santander, Banco Cental Hispano merger and Banesto and Abbey acquisitions
Citigroup	Citicorp and Travelers merger
Deutsche Bank	Bankers Trust acquisition
Dresdner	Acquired by Allianz
Fortis	Générale de Banque, Generale Bank Nederland, VSB Bank and MeesPierson aquisitions and ASLK-CGER Bank merger
HSBC	Crédit Commerciel de France, Household International and previously Midland Bank acquisitions
ING	Banque Bruxelles Lambert acquisition
JPMorgan Chase	JP Morgan and Chase Bank merger and previously Chemical Bank acquisition of Chase Bank retaining Chase brand and Bank One merger
Morgan Stanley	Dean Witter acquisition
Royal Bank of Scotland	National Westminster Bank acquisition
Société Générale	Crédit du Nord acquisition, Komercni Banka acquisition
Sumitomo Mitsui	Merger of Sumitomo Bank and Mitsui Bank
United Bank of Switzerland	Union Bank of Switzerland and Swiss Banking Corporation merger

Table 6.11 Best Banks in Business Activities 2004

Bank	Global Bank	Investment Bank	Mergers and Acquisitions	Corporate Bank	Equity	Risk Management	Asset Management	Credit Derivatives	Foreign Exchange	Global Private Bank
Citigroup		Citigroup***		Citigroup***						
Deutsche Bank						Deutsche Bank**		Deutsche Bank*	Deutsche Bank**	
Goldman Sachs			Goldman Sachs* Goldman Sachs**							
HSBC	HSBC* HSBC**									
Morgan Stanley					Morgan Stanley*				Morgan Stanley**	
UBS		UBS**			UBS**		UBS***		UBS*	UBS** UBS***

* The Banker
** Euromoney
*** Global Finance
Source: The Banker, September 2004, Euromoney, July 2004 and Global Finance, October 2004

The best bank among all banks in 10 selected banking activities is outlined in Table 6.11. This composite of those banks considered the best bank in these different business activities is compiled from polls in *The Banker, Euromoney* and *Global Finance*. There are essentially six global banks that dominate these banking activities. Three are European and three are American.

International banking based on the proportion of foreign assets of banks and their rankings in selected banking services, which represent the competitive advantages of quality and customer responsiveness, is dominated by relatively few considering the number of banks globally and these banks are from only a few countries. These countries vary in size. In these countries, with the exception of the United States which is only recently consolidating following legislation eliminating barriers to interstate banking, the banking industry is dominated by a few banks. This consolidation is a source of market power for banks and is also a catalyst for banks to become more internationally oriented. The leading banks are represented by 20 universal banks and four independent investment banks. The six banks that are considered the best bank in specific business activities consist of four universal banks and two independent investment banks. The four universal banks are ranked in Table 6.8 as having 30% or more foreign assets and are ranked in Table 6.7 among the four highest in terms of frequency of ranking by selected business activity. The two investment banks have high frequencies of ranking by selected business activity though they are considered in only eight of the ten business activities.

Part V

The Evolving International Banking Industry

7
Trends and Strategies of International Banks

The Netherlands was the leading technological country as measured by productivity and growth rates from the the early 18th century until the early 19th century. Thereafter the United Kingdom emerged as the leading technological country until the late 19th century when the United States assumed this status. In the 19th and early 20th centuries international banking was dominated by European banks, especially British and French banks and the United Kingdom and France were net creditors. American and Japanese banks were restricted from branching abroad and Germany only became unified in the late 19th century. Swiss banks were internationalised though they had few foreign branches. One of the most important innovations in technology that influenced banking was the telegraph which linked the financial centres and the periphery. The introduction of commercial satellite in the 1960s had an analogous, though much wider, effect on the banking industry and financial markets.

The integration of the world economy attained during the gold standard era was reversed during the inter-war years due to trade protectionist policies. This also had an effect on the international banking industry. The United States emerged as the leading creditor country and New York emerged as the leading international financial centre. However, it was not as international in focus as London and Amsterdam had been previously, mainly due to American investors' preferences which limited the amount of capital that was available for investment abroad. The United States government was also more focused on its own economy rather than the international economy.

The decline of London as the hegemonic financial centre may be attributed to the effects of World War I and the disintegration of the international banking networks managed by the London based private bankers. New York should have continued to be the hegemonic international financial centre once it attained this status in the 1920s. It effectively withdrew from international banking during the 1930s. It was challenged by resurgence in London due to the emergence of the euromarkets in the 1950s, and which also was the centre of finance for the sterling area, and the emergence of Japan as an industrial power in the post World War II period and of Tokyo as one of the leading international financial centres. Regulations were introduced in the United States in the 1960s that motivated its banks to establish in London and this also allowed London to re-emerge as a leading international financial centre with continental European and Japanese banks also establishing there to compete in the supranational financial markets. It is only since the mid 20th century, during the contemporary banking period, that there have been several international financial centres sharing the hegemony.

The gold standard, managed by a few countries, was superseded by the Bretton Woods fixed exchange system, and was in effect a dollar exchange standard. The United States was, during the Bretton Woods era, the world financial leader and its currency was an international reserve currency similar to the United Kingdom during the gold standard era. In the contemporary banking era there has been a closer integration of economies, economic policies and financial markets. Liberalisation of trade in banking services and deregulation of banking markets, international trade agreements, especially those specific to trade in banking services and the abandonment of exchange controls had similar integrating effects.

While banking has been liberalised and deregulated there has been a corresponding re-regulation of the industry. The response of regulators has been increased co-ordination at international and supranational levels to ensure stability in financial markets. Governments became actively involved in the regulation of the banking industry during the second half of the 19th century although in many instances they have less control on certain aspects of their economies due to the influence of banks, other financial firms and institutional investors in international financial markets.

Regulation is often the catalyst for innovation. Innovations in products and processes and the emergence of supranational markets have contributed to the increase in international banking activity and the current landscape of the industry. Many of these banking innovations would not have been possible though without the corresponding innovations in information and communications technologies. While the concepts of some derivative financial products were in use in the modern banking era it was the innovations in technology that allowed banks to manage the volume of transactions. Innovations in risk management products, credit products and deposit products have been a factor in the internationalisation of banking and financial markets.

International trade and international banking have a real and a financial aspect and while these were interdependent until the contemporary banking era they have since become decoupled, although in the late 19th century the bill on London had become a purely financial instrument. The increase in the volume of international capital flows has been greater than the increase in the volume of international trade in goods and services and most of the transactions in the foreign exchange market and in derivatives markets have no connection to international trade. The demand for capital in developing countries and emerging market economies and current account deficits in developed countries have provided banks with opportunities for international lending.

The reduction in the level of barriers to trade and foreign direct investment has allowed banks to expand internationally with relatively fewer restrictions.

Trade agreements and legislation have specified the type and range of banking services that may be provided. By allowing a broad range of services that represent commercial and investment banking services to be provided by banks, the universal banking model has emerged as the standard model. This is also evident from the acquisitions by commercial banks of investment banks and the relatively fewer number of independent international investment banks. Of course, the large capital resources of commercial banks have complemented investment banking activities. Despite the openness of banking markets there continues to exist many barriers to trade in banking services and foreign direct investment by banks, and which cannot be legislated for. These barriers are mostly implicit, such as, information asymmetries, customer loyalty and switching costs and along with geographically segmented banking markets allow domestic banks to maintain advantages over foreign banks.

Foreign banks have significant barriers to competition in terms of market share of retail banking markets. When they establish in foreign markets *de novo* they tend to focus on corporate customers. They also tend to specialise in niche market exploiting whatever competitive advantage they have over domestic banks. Indeed most developed countries are over-banked and their banking markets are highly competitive. Furthermore, non-bank financial institutions are competing with retail banks, especially in the commoditised retail banking market and consumer finance. An alternative strategy that some banks have followed has been to acquire a foreign bank with a retail network which is essentially purchasing market share. HSBC has followed this strategy in France and ABN AMRO in the United States. Citigroup and BBVA have also followed similar strategies in Mexico whereby they control the majority of the Mexican retail banking market.

Expanding internationally depends on foreign country characteristics, banking market dynamics and a bank's competitive advantages. Banks that are more efficient or have access to resources at a lower cost, such as, due to a higher credit rating, have cost advantages. Brand and reputation, achieved through the quality of products, and innovation in products, are particularly relevant due to the complex products that corporate customers demand and which is the main customer group in international banking. For banks to compete in international banking they must have superior competitive advantage in the geographic and product markets in which they compete.

Competitive advantage is possible through superior quality of and innovation in products and processes, superior efficiency in production and focusing on a customer oriented approach. To obtain these advantages banks must have the resources of quality personnel, brand and reputation, an effective and efficient infrastructure and an international network of strategically located offices although it is their capabilities in managing these that provides them with a distinctive competency. Innovation is a function of human capital and the management and culture of a bank and dynamic banks are strongly motivated to innovate when they may gain and sustain a competitive advantage.

Cost leadership in terms of lower production costs than competitors, differentiation in terms of unique products, which is difficult due to competitors introducing similar products, or unique competencies lead to competitive advantage and higher profitability. Universal banks obtain economies through related diversification. Universal banks and independent investment banks are the most common types of banks among the leading international banks. Universal banks have an advantage over investment banks in terms of available capital although investment banks through specialisation often have advantages in specific activites of investment banking.

Technology has the potential to narrow the differences between different size banks, especially in technology related services such as e-banking. This is particularly relevant to commercial banking and especially retail commercial banking where the use of technology has more potential for expanding market reach and reducing costs of production.

In most developed countries net interest margins have narrowed in recent years due to competition. This competition, consolidation and concentration in most domestic banking markets banks has motivated banks to extend their market reach to overcome the limited further business opportunities in domestic markets.

The process of consolidation in banking has occurred in different phases in countries. While there have been more mergers and acquisitions, between domestic banks and with other financial institutions in domestic markets, there has also been an increase in the volume of cross-border merger and acquisitions. Domestic mergers have the most scope for cost reduction. Some countries are so highly concentrated there is no further scope for consolidation and therefore for banks from these countries, the only options are to invest abroad or merge or acquire cross-border.

Economies of scale, or synergies, are one of the main motivating factors cited for these mergers and acquisitions. Although most studies suggest that large banks do not attain economies of scale, this has not been a deterrent to mergers and acquisition in banking. Most banks also consider that they could improve efficiency and management in an acquired bank, and in some cross-border mergers and acquisitions a motivating factor is the transfer of managerial practices. Cross selling and cross subsidising business activities are other motivations.

The banking industry in most industrialised countries tend to be oligopolistic, with a few firms dominating although many other smaller banks operate in the same market, though not maybe in the same strategic groups, and banks that dominate their domestic markets vary considerably in size between countries. Following customers and following other banks are often reasons for banks investing directly abroad. Banks tend to establish *de novo* in locations where concentration is low, as there is less competition, and potential for increasing business is high. However, they also establish their own offices in financial centres, which are highly concentrated. They do so for different reasons and are not competing only for domestic business. There is, of course, the acquired status of being located in the leading financial centres and in some other countries and the marketing of this conveys an international image.

International banking is becoming concentrated in a few large banks through mergers and acquisitions in the United States, in

Europe and in Japan and between banks from different countries and regions. Many banks are pursuing regional international policies evidenced by the geographic proximity of their mergers and acquisitions. The size of a bank influences its ability to extend geographic reach due to the constraints of resources, financial and human, and in terms of its business activities and customer base. When the costs associated with foreign direct investment are high then only potentially profitable foreign markets would attract foreign direct investment. Large banks are also capable of participating and competing in some international banking transactions that other banks are restricted from through size, such as, underwriting. They are also capable of providing a broader range of services. Mergers and acquisitions between foreign banks increases market reach and may, depending on the types of institutions, extend product reach. Those between bank and other financial institutions, such as insurance companies, increases product range and further the scope for cross selling. There could be an increase in efficiency through the transfer of distinctive competencies and superior capabilities to the acquired bank. There is also a countervailing element of culture that must be managed in cross-border mergers and acquisitions. Mergers and acquisitions, of course, may be for defensive measures especially those between banks in the same country to avoid being acquired by a foreign banks.

International capital raising has shifted from security capitalism managed by the international private bankers in the 19th and early 20th centuries to indirect financing through intermediaries to the more recent emphasis on capital markets. Disintermediation affects banks as customers circumvent the banking system and access financial markets directly. This process is partly responsible for the decline in the relative share of bank lending in international credit markets due to the issuing of short-term commercial paper and long-term bonds. As corporate customers rely more on capital markets investment banking services are of more importance and partly the reason for commercial banks developing their own investment banking divisions or acquiring investment banks.

Banks have a choice of strategies when competing in international banking between being global or regional international and whether to be in retail or wholesale banking, or both, and between the range of products and services they provide, such as commercial banking or investment banking or both. A bank may pursue a transactional approach to its business activities rather than a relationship approach, or both depending on the services and the market. While many foreign affiliates select a local bank as their choice of bank this bank is likely to be a leading international bank.

International banking has diverged from domestic banking in terms of products and services. There is also competition from other types of financial intermediaries, such as mutual funds, that are not subject to the same regulations as banks. Banks have to become more customer oriented and focus on customer retention, despite high switching costs and loyalty among customers, due to the increased competition from foreign banks especially in concentrated markets and in corporate banking activities. The organisation structure in many international banks is products or customer type based. The most common type of foreign office is a branch.

There an elite group of leading international banks from a few countries. This is similar to other industries. In terms of competition between the leading banks there are more European banks ranked among the leading banks based on the proportion of foreign assets and banking activities. Independent American investment banks are the specialists and leaders in investment banking. Despite mergers in Japanese banking and the establishment of three main banks with large amounts of assets they are less international in terms of the proportion of their assets that are foreign and are represented among the leaders in only some banking activities.

Some of the main issues for banks are profitability and increased competition. The profitability of domestic retail banking divisions of interationally focused universal banks and the increased competition from non-financial firms in this domestic retail sector is an issue that impacts on their further internationalisation. There is also the issue of the capability of universal banks to compete with specialist investment banks in certain banking activities although this must be balanced with the advantages that universal banks have in terms of capital.

Notes

Introduction

1 Goldsmith, R., Premodern Financial Systems: A Historical Comparative Study, Cambridge University Press, Cambridge, 1987, p. 3.

Chapter 1 International Banking in the Pre-Modern and Modern Banking Eras

1 Goldsmith, op. cit., p. 162.
2 Abulafia, Italian Banking in the Middle Ages, in Teichova, A., Kurgan-Van Hentenryk, G., and Ziegler, D. (eds), Banking, Trade and Industry, Europe, America and Asia from the Thirteenth to the Twentieth Century, Cambridge University Press, Cambridge, 1997, pp. 24–25.
3 Sobel, R., The Pursuit of Wealth: The Incredible Story of Money throughout the Ages, McGraw-Hill, New York, 2000, p. 47.
4 Kindleberger, C., Financial History of Western Europe, Allen and Unwin, London, 1984, p. 37 and p. 95.
5 Hoitman-de Smedt, H., The Banking System in Belgium through the Centuries, in Pöhl, K., A Handbook of European Banking History, European Association of Banking History, 1994, p. 47.
6 North, M., The Great German Banking Houses and International Merchants, Sixteenth to Nineteenth Century, in Teichova, A., Kurgan-Van Hentenryk, G., and Ziegler, D. (eds), op. cit., p. 35 and p. 38.
7 Kindleberger, 1984, op. cit., p. 45.
8 Schneider, J. and Schwarzer, O., in Fisher, W., McInnis, R.M., and Schneider, J. (eds), The Emergence of the World Economy 1500–1914, Stuttgart, pp. 18–19 and p. 150.
9 Germain, R., The International Organisation of Credit, States and Global Finance in the World-Economy, Cambridge University Press, Cambridge, 1997, pp. 36–37.
10 Kindleberger, 1984, op. cit., p. 37 and Van der Wee, H., Banking and the Rise of Capitalism in North-West Europe, in Teichova, A., Kurgan-Van Hentenryk, G., and Ziegler, D. (eds), op. cit., p. 184.
11 Kindleberger, Historical Economics, Wheatsheaf, New York, 1990, p. 277 and Goldsmith, R., op. cit., pp. 217–220.
12 Kindleberger, 1990, op. cit., pp. 214–215.
13 ibid., p. 277, Goldsmith, op. cit., p. 215, Born, K., International Banking in the Nineteenth and Twentieth Centuries, Berg, Oxford, 1983, p. 27.
14 Van der Wee, in Teichova, A., Kurgan-Van Hentenryk, G., and Ziegler, D. (eds), op. cit., p. 187.
15 Kerridge, Trade and Banking in Early Modern England, Manchester University Press, Manchester, 1992, p. 47 and p. 79 and de Cecco, M.,

Money and Empire: the International Gold Standard, 1890–1914, Blackwell, Oxford, 1974, p. 78.

16 de Cecco, op. cit., p. 85.

17 Madisson, A., The World Economy: A Millennial Perspective, Organisation for Economic Co-operation and Development, Paris, 2001.

18 Caves, R., Frankel, J., and Jones R., World Trade and Payments, Scott Foresman, IL, 1990, p. 198 and Ferguson, N., Empire, How Britain Made the Modern World, Allen Lane, 2003, pp. 242–244.

19 Pringle, R., Financial Markets and Government, WIDER Working Paper 57, World Institute for Development Economics, Helsinki, 1989.

20 Cameron, R., Banking in the Early Stages of Industrialisation, Oxford University Press, New York, 1967 p. 100.

21 Bussière, E., in Teichova, A., Kurgan-Van Hentenryk, G., and Ziegler, D. (eds), op. cit., pp. 119–124.

22 Hertner, P., in Jones, G. (ed.), Banks as Multinationals, Routledge, London, 1990, p. 102 and p. 112 and Born, op. cit., p. 134.

23 Born, op. cit., p. 123.

24 Kynaston, D., The City of London, Volume II, Golden Years 1890–1914, Pimlico, 1996, p. 126.

25 Kindleberger, 1984, op. cit., pp. 227–228 and North, in Teichova, A., Kurgan-Van Hentenryk, G., and Ziegler, D. (eds), 1997, op. cit., p. 46.

26 Cassis, Y., Banking and the Rise of Capitalism in Switzerland, in Teichova, A., Kurgan-Van Hentenryk, G., and Ziegler, D. (eds), 1997, op. cit., p. 163, Born, op. cit., p. 23, and Kindleberger, 1984, op. cit., p. 96.

27 Cassis, Y., Swiss International Banking, in Jones, G. (ed.), Banks as Multinationals, Routledge, London, 1990, p. 99 and p. 160 and Cassis, Y., Banks and Banking in Switzerland in the Nineteenth and Twentieth Centuries, in Pöhl, K., op. cit., p. 1020.

28 Cameron, op. cit., p. 111.

29 Gould, D. and Ruffin, R., What Determines Economic Growth? Federal Reserve Bank of Dallas, Economic Review, Second Quarter, 1993, Table 1, p. 26 and Webb, R., Personal Saving Behaviour and Real Economic Activity, Federal Reserve Bank of Richmond, Economic Quarterly, Volume 99–2, 1993, Table 2, p. 2 citing Madison, A., Dynamic Forces in Capitalist Development; a Long Run Comparative View, Oxford University Press, Oxford, 1991.

30 Clair, R. and Tucker, P., Interstate Banking and the Federal Reserve: A Historical Perspective, Federal Reserve Bank of Dallas, Economic Review, November 1989, p. 2.

31 Smith, R., Comeback, The Restoration of American Banking Power in the New World Economy, Harvard Business School Press, Harvard, 1993, p. 47.

32 Broadus, A., Central Banking, Then and Now, Federal Reserve Bank of Richmond, Economic Quarterly, Volume 79–2, 1993, p. 4 and Mengle, D., The Case for Interstate Branch Banking, Federal Reserve Bank of Richmond, Economic Review, Volume 76–6, 1990.

33 Ramirez, C. and De Long, J., Understanding America's Steps Toward Financial Capitalism: Politics, the Depression and the Separation of Commercial and Investment Banking, Public Choice, 106, 2001, p. 95.

34 Hayes, S. and Hubbard, P., Investment Banking, A Tale of Three Cities, Harvard Business Press, Harvard, 1990, p. 105.

35 Reynolds, D., American Globalism: Mass, Motion and the Multiplier Effect, in Hopkins, A., Globalisation in World History, Pimlico, London, 2002, p. 249.
36 Sobel, op. cit., p. 253.
37 Jones, G., (ed.), 1990, op. cit., p. 195 and Hayes and Hubbard, op. cit., p. 139.
38 Jones, A History of Multinational Banking and Financial Centres, paper presented at a Conference on Banking History, Basel, 1991, p. 14.
39 Van der Wee, H., The Onrush of Modern Globalisation in China, in Globalization in World History, in Hopkins, A., op. cit., p. 167 and Ishii, K., The Role of Banking in Japan, 1882–1973 in Teichova, A., Kurgan-Van Hentenryk, G., and Ziegler, D. (eds), op. cit., p. 408.
40 Ishii, in Teichova, A., Kurgan-Van Hentenryk, G., and Ziegler, D. (eds), 1997, op. cit., p. 404, and Hayes and Hubbard, op. cit., p. 149 and p. 156.
41 Heffernan, S., Modern Banking in Theory and Practice, Wiley, Chichester, 1996, p. 251.
42 Reed, H., The Ascent of Tokyo as an International Financial Centre, Journal of International Business Studies, Volume 11, 1980, Table 3, p. 28 and pp. 31–32.
43 The Banker, Financial Times Publications, March 1994, pp. 68–69.
44 Eichengreen, B., Globalizing Capital: A History of the International Monetary System, Princeton University Press, Princeton, 1996, p. 12.
45 Germain, op. cit., pp. 55–57.
46 Newton, L., English Banking Concentration and Internationalisation: Contemporary Debate, 1880–1920, in Kinsey, S. and Newton, L. (eds), International Banking in an Age of Transition: Globalisation, Automation, Banks and their Archives, Ashgate, Aldershot, 1998, p. 80.
47 Cottrell, P., Aspects of Commercial Banking in Northern and Central Europe, 1880–1931, in Kinsey, S., and Newton, L. (eds), op. cit., Table 10.2, p. 106.
48 Michie, R., The City of London as a Global Financial Centre, 1880–1939: Finance, Foreign Exchange and the First World War, paper presented at the Annual Conference of the European Association for Banking History, 2002.
49 Germain, op. cit., pp. 62–64.
50 Fishlow, A., in Van der Wee, H., and Aerts, E. (eds), Debates and Controversies in Economic History, Presses Universitaire de Louvain, 1990, p. 133 and p. 156. The exchange rate used to convert pounds into dollar for comparative purposes is \$4.86 to the £ as this is the rate that the United Kingdom returned to the gold exchange standard in 1925.
51 Hayes and Hubbard, op. cit., pp. 23–24.
52 Germain, op. cit., p. 66, Eichengreen, op. cit., p. 49.
53 Eichengreen, op. cit., p. 68 and pp. 70–71.
54 Kenwood, A. and Lougheed, A., The Growth of the International Economy 1820–1980, Allen and Unwin, London, 1983, p. 198.
55 Fishlow, in Van der Wee, H. and Aerts, E. (eds), op. cit., pp. 135–136.
56 Kenwood and Lougheed, op. cit., p. 198.
57 Huertas, T., US Multinational Banking: History and Prospects, in Jones, G., (ed.), 1990, op. cit., p. 252 and pp. 255–256.
58 Goldsmith, op. cit., p. 85.

59 Germain, op. cit., p. 48.
60 Born, op. cit., p. 24 and North, in Teichova, A., Kurgan-Van Hentenryk, G., and Ziegler, D. (eds), op. cit., pp. 41–42.
61 Roberts, R. and Kynaston, D., City State, a Contemporary History of the City of London and How Money Triumphed, Profile Books, 2002, Table 6.1, p. 94.
62 Born, op. cit., p. 117.
63 Jones, G., (ed.), 1990, op. cit., p. 24.
64 Hertner in Jones, G., (ed.), 1990, op. cit., p. 112.
65 Cassis, in Jones, G., (ed.), 1990, op. cit., p. 169.
66 Jones, 1991, op. cit., p. 11.
67 Huertas in Jones, 1990, op. cit., p. 252 and pp. 255–256.
68 This was the view of European bankers discussed at a meeting of the European Advisory Committee, a banking club, in 1964 and cited in Ross, D., European Banking Clubs in the 1960s: A Flawed Strategy, Business and Economic History, 27, 2, 1998, p. 361.
69 Ross, op. cit., pp. 354–355.
70 Born, op. cit., p. 308.
71 Winton, J., Lloyds Bank, Oxford University Press, Oxford, 1982, pp. 182–183.
72 Schenk, C., The Rise of Hong Kong and Tokyo as International Financial Centres after 1950, paper presented at the Annual Conference of the European Association for Banking History, 2002, p. 11.
73 Kynaston, The City of London, Volume IV, 1945–2000, a Club No More, Pimlico, London, 2002, p. 502.
74 Aliber, R., International Banking: a Survey, Journal of Money, Credit and Banking, Volume XVI, Number 4, Part 2, November 1984, p. 689.

Chapter 2 Contemporary International Banking Markets

1 Hertner, P., in Jones, 1990., op. cit., p. 99.
2 Ferguson, op. cit., p. 354.
3 Gould and Ruffin, op. cit., Table 1, p. 26.
4 Kynaston, 2002, op. cit., p. 403.
5 Roberts and Kynaston, op. cit., p. 88 and p. 91.
6 Hayes and Hubbard, op. cit., pp. 73–74 and p. 302.
7 Kynaston, 2002, op. cit., p. 403.
8 Houpt, J., International Trends for US Banks and Banking Markets, Board of Governors of the Federal Reserve System, 1988, p. 7, and Huertas, in Jones, G., (ed.), 1990, op. cit., pp. 253–254.
9 Bank for International Settlements, International Banking and Financial Market Developments, February 1997, p. 22.
10 Germain, op. cit., p. 85.
11 Kynaston, 2002, op. cit., p. 276.
12 Hayes and Hubbard, op. cit., pp. 32–33.
13 Kynaston, 2002, op. cit., p. 279 and p. 551.
14 Scott-Quinn, B., US Investment Banks as Multinationals, in Jones, G., (ed.), 1990, op. cit., p. 280.

15 Kynaston, 2002, op. cit., p. 324.
16 Ibid., pp. 548–551.
17 Hayes and Hubbard, op. cit., p. 48 and p. 52.
18 Bank for International Settlements, Triennial Central Bank Survey of Foreign Exchange and Derivatives Market Activity in April 2004, Preliminary Global Results, September 2004, Table 2, p. 10 and Table 3, p. 11.
19 World's Best Foreign Exchange Banks 2005, Global Finance, January 2005.
20 Napoli, J., Derivative Markets and Competitiveness, Federal Reserve Bank of Chicago Economic Perspectives, Volume XVI, Issue 4, 1992, p. 14 and p. 23.
21 Becketti, S., Are Derivatives Too Risky for Banks?, Federal Reserve Bank of Kansas City Economic Review, Volume 78, Number 73, 1993, p. 29.
22 Siems, T., Financial Derivatives: Are New Regulations Warranted? Federal Reserve Bank of Dallas, Financial Industry Studies, August 1994, p. 6 and p. 10.
23 Duca, J., Regulation, Bank Competitiveness and Episodes of Missing Money, Federal Reserve Bank of Dallas Economic Review, Second Quarter, 1993, p. 6.
24 Hahn, T., Commercial Paper, Federal Reserve Bank of Richmond Economic Quarterly, Volume 79, Number 2, 1993, p. 49.
25 UCITS, Undertakings for Collective Investments in Transferable Securities, or SICAV, Société d'Investissements à Captial Variable.
26 Sobel, op. cit., pp. 304–305.
27 Sellon, G., Changes in Financial Intermediation: The Role of Pension and Mutual Funds, Federal Reserve Bank of Kansas City Economic Review, Volume 77, Number 3, 1992, p. 61.
28 Hahn, op. cit., p. 49.
29 Bank for International Settlements, International Banking and Financial Market Developments, August 1991.
30 Bank for International Settlements, Quarterly Review, June 2004, Table 13 A, p. A 86.
31 Duca, J., How Low Interest Rates Impact Financial Institutions, Federal Reserve Bank of Dallas, Southwest Economy, Issue 6, 2003, p. 9.
32 Hilton, A., Sterling Money Market Funds, Bank of England Quarterly Bulletin, Summer 2004, Chart 1, p. 176, Chart 2, p. 177, Chart 5, p. 179 and Chart A and Chart B, p. 180.
33 Madisson, 2001, op. cit., Table 3–3, p. 128 and Sargent, T., in Aliber, 1984, op. cit., p. 20.
34 McKinsey Global Institute, The Global Capital Market: Supply, Pricing and Allocation, Financial Institutions Group, 1994, Chapter 2, Exhibit 7.
35 Woodridge, P., Domanski, D., and Cobau, A., Changing Links between Mature and Emerging Financial Markets, Bank for International Settlements Quarterly Review, September 2003, p. 48.
36 United Nations Conference on Trade and Development, Trade and Development Report, New York and Geneva, 2004, p. 57 and Table 2.5, p. 58.
37 United Nations Conference on Trade and Development, World Investment Report, New York and Geneva, 2004, Tables III.1, p. 99, III.2, p. 100, III.11, p. 128 and A.III.4, p. 321.
38 Wezel, T., Foreign Bank Entry into Emerging Economies,: An Empirical Assessment of the Determinants and Risks Predicated on German FDI Data, Discussion Paper 1/2004, Series 1, Studies of the Economic Research Centre, Deutsche Bundesbank, 2004, Figure 1, p. 18.

Chapter 3 Regulation, Trade Agreements, Consolidation and Integration in International Banking

1 Mikdashi, Z., Whither Financial Intermediation, in Mikdashi, Z. (ed.), Financial Intermediation in the 21st Century, Palgrave, 2001, p. 258.
2 Plessis, A., The History of Banks in France, in Pöhl, K., op. cit., p. 193.
3 Kynaston, 2004, op. cit., p. 448.
4 Kashyap, A. and Stein, J., Cyclical Implications of the Basel II Capital Standards, Federal Reserve Bank of Chicago, Economic Perspectives, First Quarter 2004, p. 19.
5 Roever, W. and Fabozzi, F., A Primer on Securitization, Journal of Structured and Project Finance, Volume 9, Issue 2, 2003, p. 5.
6 Bank for International Settlements, High Level Principles for the Cross-border Implementation of the New Accord, Basel Committee on Banking Supervision, 2003.
7 The Banker, Radley Survey, Basel II supplement, October, 2003.
8 Kashyap and Stein, op. cit., p. 18.
9 European Commission, The Single Market Review Series, Subseries II – Impact on Services, Credit Institutions and Banking, 1997.
10 Sauvé, P. and Gozales-Hermosillo, B., Implications of the NAFTA for Canadian Financial Institutions, The NAFTA Papers, C.D. Howe Institute Commentary, Number 44, April 1993.
11 For an outline of the alternative methods of regulation of securities business refer to the discussion in Pan, E., Harmonisation of US-EU Securities Regulation: the Case for a Single European Regulator, Law and Policy in International Business, 34, 2, 2004.
12 Belaisch, A., Kodres, L., Levy, J., and Ubide, A., Euro-Area Banking at the Crossroads, Working Paper WP/01/28, International Monetary Fund, 2001, Table 2, p. 8 and p. 9.
13 Bank of England, Cross-border Alliances in Banking and Financial Services in the Single Market Quarterly Bulletin, August 1993, p. 374.
14 Brewer, E., Jackson, W., Jagtiani, J., and Nguyen, T., The Price of Bank Mergers in the 1990s, Federal Reserve Bank of Chicago, Economic Perspectives, Quarter 1, 2000, p. 2, and Table 1, p. 5.
15 Gunther, J. and Moore, R., Small Banks' Competitors Loom Large, Federal Reserve Bank of Dallas, Southwest Economy, Issue 1, 2004, pp. 9–10.
16 Amel D., Barnes, C., Panetta, F., and Salleo, C., Consolidation and Efficiency in the Financial Sector: A Review of the International Evidence, Banca d'Italia, Temi di Discussione del Servizio Studi, Number 464, 2002, p. 9.
17 Berger, A., Buch, C., De Long, G., and De Young, R., Exporting Financial Institutions Management via Foreign Direct Investment Mergers and Acquisitions, Journal of International Money and Finance, 23, 2004, Table 1 p. 345. A reason for the large number mergers and acquisitions is that all public and private corporate transactions involving at least 5% of the purchased company are included in the data. Nonetheless the data illustrates the trends in these mergers and acquisitions.
18 Ibid., Table 2, p. 345 and Figure 3, p. 343.
19 Bank for International Settlements, Committee on the Global Financial System, Foreign Direct Investment in the Financial Sector of Emerging Market Economies, 2004, Graph 1, p. 4, Graph 2, p. 5, and p. 28.

20 Banking Beyond Frontiers: Will European Consumers Buy It? KPMG, March 2004.
21 Retail Bank of the Future, The Banker and Henrion Ludlow Schmidt Survey, The Banker, June 2003.
22 Bank for International Settlements, Management and Supervision of Cross-Border Electronic Banking Activities, 2003, p. 4 and Annex I, p. 12.
23 Schaechter, A., Issues in Electronic Banking: an Overview, Policy Discussion Paper, PDP/02/6, International Monetary Fund, 2002, p. 4 and p. 6.
24 Global Finance, The World's Best Internet Banks, September 2004.

Chapter 4 Trade Theories and International Banking

1 Hindley, B. and Smith, A., Comparative Advantage in Trade in Services, World Economy, 7, 1984, p. 386.
2 ibid., p. 374.
3 Arndt, H., Comparative Advantage in Trade in Financial Services, Banca Nazionale del Lavoro, Quarterly Review, March, 1988, p. 73.
4 Hanweck, G. and Shull, B., The Bank Merger Movement: Efficiency, Stability and Competitive Policy Concerns, Antitrust Bulletin, Volume 44, 1999, pp. 261–262.
5 Arndt, op. cit., p. 61.
6 Feketekuty, G., in Walter, I. and Murray, T. (eds), Handbook of International Business, Wiley, New York, 1988, p. 23.8 and pp. 23.26.
7 Jones, R. and Ruane, F., Options for Trade in Services, Oxford Economic Papers, 42, 1990, p. 673.
8 Feketekuty, G., in Walter, I. and Murray, T., op. cit., pp. 23.15.
9 Aliber, R., Towards a Theory of International Banking, Federal Reserve Bank of San Francisco, Spring 1976, p. 5 and Aliber, 1984, op. cit., p. 661.
10 Gray, J. and Gray, H., The Multinational Bank: a Financial MNC? Journal of Banking and Finance, 5, 1981.
11 Casson, M., The Economic Theory of Multinational Banking, an Internalisation Approach, University of Reading, Department of Economics Discussion Paper in International Investment and Business Studies, Volume II, Number 133, 1989.
12 Ter Wengel, J., International Trade in Banking Services, Journal of International Money and Finance, Volume 14, Issue 1, 1995.
13 Berger, et al., 2004, p. 340 and p. 362.
14 Tori, C. and Tori, S., Exchange Market Pressure, Trade, Sovereign Credit Ratings and United States' Exports of Banking Services Atlantic Economic Journal, Volume 29, Number 1, 2001.
15 Li, D., Moshirian, F., and Sim, A., The Determinants of Intra-industry Trade in Insurance Services, Journal of Risk and Insurance, June, 2003.
16 Barth, J., Caprio, G., and Levine, R., The Regulation and Supervision of Banks Around the World: a New Database, Policy Research Working Paper 2588, World Bank, Development Economics Department, Washington, cited in Foreign Bank Entry: Experience, Implications for Developing Economies, and Agenda for Further Research, Clarke, G., Cull, R., Soledad Martinez Peria, M., and Sanches, S., The World Bank Research Observer, 18, 1, spring 2003, pp. 30–33.

17 Bryant, R., International Financial Intermediation, Brookings Institution, Washington, 1987, p. 63.
18 Berger, A., Dai, Q., Ongena, S., and Smith D., To What Extent will the Banking Industry be Globalised? A Study of Bank Nationality and Reach in 20 European Nations, Journal of Banking and Finance, 27, Issues 3, 2003, pp. 389–394.
19 Mutinelli, M. and Piscitello, L., Foreign Direct Investment in the Banking Sector: the case of Italian Banks in the 1990s, International Business Review, 10, 2001, pp. 668–669.
20 Gentle, C., The Titans Take Hold, How Offshoring has Changed the Competitive Dynamic for Global Financial Services Institutions, Global Financial Services Industry Group, Deloitte Touche Tohmatsu, 2004, p. 3.
21 United Nations Conference on Trade and Development, World Investment Report, New York and Geneva, 2004, Table III.13, p. 132.

Chapter 5 The Scope of International Banking, Business Activities and Markets

1 United Nations, Manual on Statistics on International Trade in Services, Department of Economic and Social Affairs, Statistical Papers 82, 2002, pp. 8, 55, 171.
2 Aliber, 1984, op. cit., p. 661.
3 Casson, 1989, op. cit., p. 4
4 Goodman, A., in Aliber, 1984, op. cit., p. 679.
5 Lewis, M. and Davis, K., Domestic and International Banking, Philips-Allan, Oxford, 1987, p. 220.
6 Yannopoulos, G., The Growth of Transnational Banking, in Casson, M., The Growth of International Business, Allen and Unwin, London, 1983, p. 236.
7 Jones, 1991, A History of Multinational Banking and Financial Centres, paper presented, Basle, 1991, p. 4.
8 Ruane, F., Comment on Neu, C., in Baldwin, R., Hamilton, C., and Sapir, A., Issues in US-EC Trade Relations, University of Chicago Press, Chicago, 1989, p. 271.
9 Neu, C., in Baldwin, R., Hamilton, C., and Sapir, A., Issues in US-EC Trade Relations, University of Chicago Press, Chicago, 1989, p. 255.
10 Grubel, H., A Theory of Multinational Banking, Banca Nazionale del Lavoro Quarterly Review, December, 1977, p. 349.
11 United Nations, Transnational Corporations in World Development, New York, 1988.
12 Casson, 1989, op. cit., Jones, 1991, op. cit., and Gray and Gray, 1981 op. cit.
13 Ankrom, R., The Corporate Bank, Sloan Management Review, 35, 2, 1994.
14 Anand, B., and Galetovic, A., Investment Banking and Security Market Development: Does Finance Follow Industry?, International Monetary Fund Working Paper, WP/01/90, 2001, pp. 6–7.
15 Hayes and Hubbard, op. cit., pp. 74, 106.
16 Eccles, R. and Crane, D., Managing through Networks in Investment Banking, California Management Review, Fall 1987, pp. 176–179.
17 Bank for International Settlements, Basel Committee on Banking Supervision, Shell Banks and Booking Offices, 2003.

18 HSBC Holdings plc, Annual Report, 2003.
19 Barclays Bank, Annual Report, 2003.
20 Deutsche Bank, Annual Report 2003.
21 United Bank of Switzerland, Annual Report, 2003.
22 Citigroup Inc, Annual Report, 2003 and Form 10-K, 2003.
23 JPMorgan Chase, Annual Report, 2003.
24 Goldman Sachs Group, Annual Report, 2003.
25 Mizuho Financial Group, Annual Report, 2003.
26 Bank for International Settlements, International Banking and Financial Market Developments, February, 1996, p. 5.

Index

Page numbers in *italics* refer to illustrations